***Praise for* Curating Your Life**

"*Curating Your Life* is not for those looking for a simple, easy life hack that will allow them to do more, better, in less time (while looking fabulous). In this smart, helpful guide, Gail Golden exposes the futility of trying to do and have it all—encouraging us instead to achieve greater harmony, fulfillment, and effectiveness through reflection and intentional choices."—**David Mooney, CEO, Alliant Credit Union**

"Gail Golden has created a masterpiece for busy people who want more meaning in their lives. She draws on her background in psychology and business to teach us how to 'curate' our lives in a purposeful way. She artfully highlights the cardinal mistakes people can't help but make and empowers us to sort out what's most important in life and use our energy for that. If you're beyond busy, this is a must-read."—**David Grossman, leadership and communications expert, founder and CEO, the Grossman Group**

"Gail Golden shows us the pathways to focusing our energy to be both more productive and more fulfilled."—**Andy Polansky, chairman and CEO, Interpublic's Constituency Management Group, and executive chairman, Weber Shandwick**

"Gail Golden provides a new prism to look through to address the work-life balance challenge facing leaders in a world with ever-increasing demands on their time. It's a highly engaging read that will inspire you to curate your life."—**Pamela Forbes Lieberman, corporate director and former CEO, True Value Company**

"*Curating Your Life* provides a candid and validating compilation of the hidden and conscious views of what it means to be human and the continuous aspirations we share to bring balance and self-awareness to our lives. Refreshing and honest."—**Ellen Rozelle Turner, president and CEO, William Everett Group**

"Finally, a book that dispenses with clichés about having it all and work-life balance. Golden translates her years of experience into a helpful guide for curating the life we want. She shows us how to maximize our potential by focusing on what's really important and casting aside the distractions that deplete energy and focus. A must-read for anyone trying and failing to be a Superwoman."—**Karen Horting, executive director and CEO, Society of Women Engineers**

"Gail Golden's *Curating Your Life* is revelatory, sound, and balanced. Too many of us have felt periods of over-obligation and inadequate self-care that require acknowledgment and action. Golden's idea of curation is both thoughtful and ruthless and provides a perspective not found frequently in a busy life. A must-read for CEOs, achievers, and passionate leaders—'a well curated life is doable.'"—**Heather Becker, CEO, the Conservation Center**

CURATING YOUR LIFE

CURATING YOUR LIFE

Ending the Struggle for Work-Life Balance

Gail Golden

ROWMAN & LITTLEFIELD
Lanham • Boulder • New York • London

Published by Rowman & Littlefield
An imprint of The Rowman & Littlefield Publishing Group, Inc.
4501 Forbes Boulevard, Suite 200, Lanham, Maryland 20706
www.rowman.com

6 Tinworth Street, London SE11 5AL, United Kingdom

British Library Cataloguing in Publication Information Available

Library of Congress Control Number: 2019038955
ISBN 978-1-5381-3287-6 (hardback : alk. paper)
ISBN 978-1-5381-3288-3 (electronic)

♾ ™ The paper used in this publication meets the minimum requirements of American National Standard for Information Sciences Perma-
nence of Paper for Printed Library Materials, ANSI/NISO Z39.48-1992.

To my thousands of clients, who taught me almost everything I know about helping, to my marvelous sons, and to Daniel Golden, the love of my life.

CONTENTS

I

DON'T BALANCE, CURATE

When I ride the train to my office in the morning, I look at the faces of the other passengers. Some sleep, most text or listen to music, and others stare dully out of the window. Almost no one looks happy, or energized, or enthusiastic.

When I walk around downtown, it's the same picture. Most people charge along, heads down or looking careworn and weary. The panhandlers on the street corners look especially miserable. But honestly, most of us don't look much happier than they do.

At the end of the day, we're heading home, the lucky ones among us to spend time with the people we love. Do we look eager and anticipatory? No. We mostly look even more tired than we did in the morning.

This is not how I want my life to be—and not yours, either.

Every day we read more articles about work-life balance, about managing your time, about having it all. Frankly, those articles mostly make us feel worse about ourselves. It's all so simple—just use the right app, drink the right juice, say the right mantra, and you too can have the perfect life. Well, I've never found life to be simple, and I'm deeply suspicious of simple answers to complicated problems.

It really is frustrating. There are so many companies offering us magical answers to all our difficulties. Just take a look at your mail—email or snail mail. Mine is full of quick solutions to make me rich, youthful, and thin. Check out the ads on TV, in publications, and on the sidebars of the websites you visit. More magic! Lately, I seem to have made it onto a sucker list for companies offering to vastly increase my client list, my income, and the number of people who are going to read this book. These offers are all magic in one way—they are excellent at reducing the weight of your wallet and making someone else rich.

I especially resent deceptively simple answers to complicated life issues. One of my pet peeves is the phrase, "Just do the right thing." You know, most of us want to do the right thing most of the time. But how do you know what the right thing is? Sometimes we differ from each other about what is right.

So I will never tell you that achieving a happy and productive life is simple. If it were, we'd all be doing it. But I know for a fact that achieving a happy and productive life *is* possible. I have spent my life and my career so far working on this problem, and in this book I will share with you what I have learned.

Early in my career, I was running my clinical psychology practice, teaching a huge lecture course at the local university, writing a weekly newspaper column, raising three little boys, trying to be a good partner to my husband, and so on and so on. I'm a high-energy person, but a lot of the time I was running on fumes. It seemed to me that I was doing none of it very well. I looked at other people who appeared to have it all together. There was the prominent physician who was also writing books, raising three kids, and serving as a leader in our synagogue. There was the professor who was doing cutting-edge research, raising four kids, writing poetry, and learning to play the guitar. There was the brilliant, highly respected therapist with the magnificent home, always impeccably dressed and beautiful. And then there was me.

How were they doing it? I used to torture myself with the image of the person I thought I should be—always calm and pleasant, on top of all my responsibilities and still having time to be loving and funny and available to others.

And then one day I had a huge revelation. *I realized that other people were looking at me as one of those people doing it all.* I was dumbfounded. Didn't they know what a train wreck I was? Wasn't it obvious?

This led me to revelation number two. *Nobody is doing it all.* Everyone cuts corners somewhere. Some of us are just better than others at hiding our "dirty little secrets."

And here's revelation number three. *Most of us make the cardinal mistake of comparing our own insides to other people's outsides.* Those folks who look as if they have it all together? Inside, they're just as freaked out, overworked, and self-critical as you are.

Some people say you just shouldn't compare yourself to others at all. Have your own standards and don't pay any attention to how others are doing. Frankly, I don't buy that for one second. Human beings are social animals, and I have never met a person who doesn't incorporate information about other people into his or her self-evaluation. I think that's just another impossible goal for us to fail at.

Is it helpful to compare yourself to others? Does it inspire you to work harder or make you feel discouraged? How do you choose with whom you will compare yourself? Psychologists have done a lot of research on how people use social comparison. For example, one study looked at what happens if you compare yourself to others who are doing worse than you vs. others who are doing better. You might think this is simple—comparing yourself with others who are worse off will make you feel better about yourself. (I used to joke that I preferred to hang around only with people who were older, fatter, and poorer than me. That way I got to feel young, slim, and rich.) On the other hand, you might predict that if you compare yourself to people who are doing better than you, you will feel worse about yourself.

Turns out it's not quite that simple. (As I said before, life rarely is.) How comparisons make us feel doesn't just depend on whether we're comparing up or down. It also depends on whether we think that we could move toward where the other person is. So if I look at someone who is more successful than me and think, "I could do that, too," the comparison could make me feel positive and energized. But if I think, "I'm such a loser, I can never be like that," I'm probably going to feel pretty crappy. On the other side of the coin, if I look at someone who is less successful than me and think, "Wow, I'm in a pretty good place," I'll feel good. But if I look at that person and think, "Yikes, my situation is pretty precarious—I could end up like that guy," then I'm not going to feel so great. [1]

The point is that almost all of us will use social comparison as one way of measuring how well we're doing. The trick is to observe others and then think about that information in ways that propel us toward great success and satisfaction. In the coming chapters, we'll talk a lot more about how to develop thought patterns that help you to lead a richer, more fulfilling life.

To review, let's go back to my three revelations:

- In spite of my feelings of inadequacy, other people thought I was someone who was doing it all.
- Nobody is doing it all.
- Most of us are making the cardinal mistake of comparing our own insides to other people's outsides. We think that because other people *look* all put together, they must *feel* all put together.

All these learnings happened in the first half of my career, when I was a psychotherapist. I spent many years deeply involved in working with unhappy people to help them create better lives for themselves. My clients included people who were depressed, anxious, obsessive-compulsive, phobic, divorcing, injured, abused, schizophrenic—the list goes on and on. The work was very hard and very satisfying and I loved it.

But after twenty-plus years, I was sitting with a new client one day as he told me about his problems and why he had come to see me. And I thought to myself, "I know you. I know what you're going to say and I know what I'm going to say. I know how long this is going to take and I know how it's going to turn out." That was the day I realized it was time for me to find a new line of work. My clients deserved a therapist who was fully engaged and I deserved to have work that challenged and excited me. The truth was, I was burned out as a therapist.

So I went looking for something else psychologists could do, and I got very intrigued with how I could help business executives do their jobs better. It seemed to me I could apply what I had learned about human behavior to a new set of problems and challenges. And if I could help one business leader do his or her job better, I would probably affect more people's emotional well-being than if I spent hundreds of hours with individual therapy clients.

It turned out that research supported my view. The field of industrial/organizational (I/O) psychology is as old as clinical psychology. I/O psychologists apply the science of human behavior to organizations and individuals in their workplaces. They focus on increasing organizational success by creating environments that get the best out of everyone who works there. The American Psychological Association has published a whole handbook on how elements of the workplace affect employees' health and well-being.[2]

There is a fascinating body of research on the impact of leadership styles on employees' productivity and happiness. For example, some researchers have looked at the impact of "transformational leadership." This leadership style is characterized by four dimensions: idealized influence, inspirational motivation, intellectual stimulation, and individualized consideration. A number of studies have demonstrated that transformational leadership has very positive effects on employee well-being, including both positive emotions and general mental health.[3]

So there was ample evidence for my notion that by using psychology to help business executives become better leaders, I would also be positively affecting the people in their organizations. (We'll explore more about how leaders and managers can create an environment that enhances productivity and joy in chapter 7.)

There was just one catch to my career plan—I didn't know beans about business. I had run my own practice, which I didn't even think of as a business. I had worked in medical and academic settings. But what did I know of corporate leadership? I imagined myself walking into a CEO's office and saying, "Hello, I'm Dr. Golden and I'm here to help you." He would respond, "What do you know of my world?" And I would have no answer.

That's why I went to business school. For two years, I ran my full-time practice and also went to school full-time. Those were the two busiest years of my life, and later on in chapter 3 I'll tell you some of the secrets of how I did it. I loved my MBA program. It blew my head right open with new ideas and challenged some of my deeply held beliefs. As a result, I have become a great fan of doing something mid-career that knocks your socks off.

MBA in hand, I said good-bye to my therapy clients (which, by the way, was quite painful for me) and joined a global management psychology consulting firm. The first year in my new career was brutal. I knew I would have to climb a learning curve, but I had no idea how hard it would be. But after a while, I began to notice something very interesting.

My new clients were very different from my old ones in many ways. In general, they were wealthier, healthier, more emotionally stable, and able to access much stronger support systems around them. But I came to realize that the two client groups were also alike in many ways—overworked, overstressed, lonely, self-critical, and exhausted, both physically and emotionally. Those captains of industry? In contrast to their mighty outsides, their insides were much the same as everyone else's.

Let me give you two examples. In 2002, one of my therapy clients was Kelly. (All client names and identifying information in this book have been disguised.) Kelly was married, ran a small business, and was raising two young children. About a year before she came to see me, Kelly started having a series of physical and cognitive symptoms. Her body felt achy and fatigued all the time. She had difficulty concentrating on her work. Even though she was tired, she had trouble sleeping. She was finding it more and more difficult to carry on with her normal schedule of responsibilities.

She went to see her primary-care doctor time and again. Her doctor ran various tests but could find no reason for Kelly's symptoms. In those days many of my referrals came from primary-care physicians, and Kelly's doctor sent her to see me. As we explored her life landscape, we realized Kelly had ignored her symptoms of fatigue and exhaustion for years. Her philosophy was to just keep on pushing through. And finally her body forced her to stop.

Second example: I met Sean in 2017 when he was referred to me for coaching by his CEO. Sean was a highly successful top-level executive who was in the running to become the next CEO of his company. He was very intelligent, hardworking, ambitious, and liked and respected by his colleagues. He had recently been given a much larger scope of responsibility and was now managing almost half the company's business. The CEO had given Sean challenging stretch goals for growing his part of the business. At home, Sean had two small children and a third on the way. The CEO was concerned that Sean was having difficulty prioritizing his work. He spent too much time on details and not enough on making himself available to his team. When I spoke with Sean, he was beginning to have doubts about whether he wanted to take on the CEO role.

On the surface, Kelly and Sean were very different people. But underneath—much the same. Both of them were trying to do too much. They were holding themselves to unreasonable standards. They were failing to listen to their bodies and their emotions. They were excessively worried about other people's standards. As a result, both of these high-potential people were at risk of failing to live the full, productive lives they were capable of leading.

I left the global consulting firm in 2009 to start my own management psychology business. I'm still loving my work and learning cool new stuff every day. And I continue to find that the themes of over-obligation, unreasonable expectations, and inadequate self-care come up over and over again as I work with my clients.

Over more than twenty-five years of helping over-burdened people, I have learned that it's all about *managing your energy* so you can lead your most joyful, productive, liberated life. Take a minute to think about energy the way an engineer does. In order to maximize your usable energy, you have to pay attention to two things. First, you have to increase your energy capacity, the amount of energy you have to work with. Second, you have to channel the outflow so you are focusing your finite amount of energy on the things that really matter and not wasting it on stupid stuff. That's what *Curating Your Life* is about.

How do you increase your energy capacity? That topic has been beautifully covered in a wonderful book, *The Power of Full Engagement*, by Jim Loehr and Tony Schwartz.[4] If you want to lead a happier, more productive life, your first assignment is to read and study that book. It changed my life and I have recommended it to almost every one of my coaching clients. Here are some of Loehr and Schwartz's key findings:

- You can't manage time. You get twenty-four hours a day and there's nothing you can do about it. Don't focus on managing time, focus on managing your energy.
- Ignore the people who tell you that life is a marathon. The most productive people know that life is not a marathon, it's a series of sprints.
- Live your life like an athlete. Sprint for a defined period of time and then take time to recover.
- Build your own personal rituals for recovery into the rhythm of your life.
- There are four kinds of energy: physical, emotional, mental, and spiritual. You need to assess and manage all four.

This brief summary doesn't begin to do justice to Loehr and Schwartz's work. *Read their book*.

One of the key lessons of *The Power of Full Engagement* is that people need to take breaks in order to manage their energy for maximum productivity. To sustain full engagement, you need to take a recovery break every 90 to 120 minutes. I don't know how fast you read, but I'm going to suggest that you take breaks from time to time as you read this book.

So how about it—want to stand up, stretch, walk around a little, have a glass of water, and then continue reading?

Maximizing your energy capacity is key to living a full and productive life. But here's the problem—these practices *take* time and energy, especially at first. Rituals for recovery? Getting enough sleep? Eating healthy meals? Taking all your vacation days? Who has the time to do all that?

Even if you follow all the wise suggestions in *The Power of Full Engagement*, you will still have a finite amount of energy. That's so important I'm going to repeat it: *No matter what you do, you will have a finite amount of energy.* And yet so many of us act as if our energy is infinite. We think we can keep adding activities and commitments to our lives and somehow we will manage to juggle it all. That's the fallacy of work-life balance. There is a real, physical limit to what even a high-energy person can do.

Some people respond to this impossible challenge by shutting down—by leading low-energy, unsatisfying lives because they feel so overwhelmed by the multiple challenges and demands that they and others place on them. (More about this is in chapter 6.) But most of the people I work with are on the other end of this spectrum—driving themselves nuts by trying to do too much.

Here's one of my favorite images for this dilemma. You have a stovetop with four burners. How many pots can you cook at one time? This is not a trick question—the answer is four. What do you have to do if you need to cook a fifth pot? Again, not a trick question—you have to take one of the pots off the stove to make room for the new one. What happens if you try to cook seventeen pots on your stove at one time? Nothing cooks properly and you end up with a huge mess on the floor.

Yet cooking seventeen pots on a four-burner stove is what so many of us try to do every day. We somehow believe we can stretch our energy capacity more and more to accommodate a ridiculous number of activities. And then we wonder why *we* become a mess on the floor!

Overworking yourself is a real, documented problem. In a review of the literature in 2009, Ronald Burke documented the disastrous consequences of working beyond your endurance:

- psychological problems
- physical health challenges
- family dysfunction
- chronic guilt
- reduced productivity
- sleep disorders
- increased accidents, both on the job and driving home from work

In Japanese there is a word, *karoshi*, that means death from overwork. Researchers have specified the number of hours of consecutive and total work time it takes to cause such a death. Contrary to the old saying, hard work has in fact killed lots of people.[5]

If you don't want to die from overwork, or for that matter experience any of the other negative consequences on this list, what can you do? How do you find the energy to do the things that matter? How do you find the energy to maximize your energy? To make it happen, you have to channel the *outflow* of your energy by *Curating Your Life*.

The verb *curate* means to select and organize something—for example, a collection, an exhibit, a library, or a performance. Think about an art exhibition. Do you think the designer of the exhibition hung every painting the museum owns on the walls? Of course not. The designer—the curator—selected the works that were most important for the theme of the exhibit and arranged them for maximum impact for the viewer. The most important works were displayed very prominently and featured on the poster for the exhibit. Less important but still relevant paintings were displayed in side rooms. What happened to the paintings that were not selected? They weren't thrown out or destroyed—just stored in the back room, perhaps for exhibit at a later date.

The curator has a very difficult job, because there are always more paintings, or books, or songs than can fit into an exhibit, a library, or a concert. It's hard because *all* the paintings, books, and songs are wonderful, yet you can't include them all. The curator needs to be both thoughtful and ruthless as she decides what stays in and what is excluded.

You know what good curation looks like. You can see it when you walk into someone's home, or read a well-designed menu or wine list, or enjoy a really well-organized conference. Take a look at figure 1.1—you won't have any trouble picking out the well-curated collection.

You can use the same process to curate your life. It means selecting those activities that are most important, meaningful, and joyful for you and focusing your energy on those endeavors. It means putting some activities in the side rooms, where they are included in your life but not featured. It also means putting a whole bunch of stuff in the back room, to be reconsidered at another time.

Curating your life means sorting your activities into three categories:

1. the things you are *not going to do*, at least not right now
2. the things you will be *mediocre* at
3. the things you will be *great* at

This is not simple. I want to emphasize that. As I said before, life is complicated, so beware of simple answers. Curating your life is a challenging, ongoing discipline that requires a whole bunch of skills. A well-curated life doesn't stay the same, any more than a museum always has the same exhibits on its walls.

This is not touchy-feely. Curating your life is about getting ahead, accomplishment, productivity, and having an impact. And it's also about happiness and well-being. The two go together.

Figure 1.1.   What curation looks like. https://www.pexels.com.

The payoff for curating your life is amazing. Living a well-curated life is *doable*. You get to feel good about yourself because you are succeeding at the things that really matter to you. You do a whole bunch of productive work and you still get to enjoy life.

I will warn you up front—curating your life can have an expected consequence. My client Joseph is a good example. Joseph was a young CEO who came to me for performance coaching. He was an exceptionally intelligent strategic thinker and innovator who was building a very successful marketing company. But Joseph's life was constant chaos. He was working until late at night, handling crisis after crisis. He was emotionally reactive, often making difficult situations worse with his intense responses. He realized his leadership style was not just unsustainable, it was diminishing his performance.

Coaching Joseph was a highly charged experience. To harness his intelligence, he had to learn to manage his energy. I trained him to recognize and control his emotions before they derailed him. Within a few months, Joseph and I found ways for him to work in a more focused, impactful manner. And then one day, Joseph presented me with a surprising new problem.

His work flow was manageable. The emotional temperature in the office was reasonably mellow. And Joseph had no idea what to do with himself.

You may be thinking, "That's a problem? It's a problem I'd like to have!" But many high-energy executives thrive in high-demand, tight-deadline situations. Some leaders are so dependent on that kind of adrenaline that they unconsciously create crises, much to the dismay of their teams.

Performance coaching is not just about learning to manage through hysterical times. It is also about learning to manage through tranquil times. So Joseph and I talked about how to navigate a lull. We identified three very important activities he could focus on in the calm times: strategic planning, developing talent on his team, and recharging. Joseph learned how to curate his life to maximize his performance during both the crazy times and the calm times.

Those people I mentioned earlier, the ones who seemed to be doing it all? Of course they weren't. But they *were* leading curated lives, focused on the activities where they wanted to be great. No one gets this right all the time, but you can learn to do it better.

Let's get started.

KEY TAKEAWAYS

- There's a good chance that other people think you are doing it all.
- Nobody is doing it all.
- Don't compare your insides to other people's outsides. Those people who look as if they have it all together? They're just especially good at hiding how flustered they are.
- Focus on managing your energy, not on managing time. That means increasing your energy capacity and then focusing it on the right things.
- Read *The Power of Full Engagement* by Loehr and Schwartz to learn how to increase your energy capacity.
- No matter what you do, you will have a finite amount of energy. Don't try to cook seventeen pots on a four-burner stove.
- Curate your life by sorting your activities into three categories:

    - the things you are not going to do, at least not right now
    - the things you will be mediocre at
    - the things you will be great at

- Curating your life is not simple.

2

DECIDE WHAT'S IMPORTANT

Let's think about our friend the museum curator. His boss, the museum director, comes to him and says, "I want you to curate an outstanding new exhibit for the museum next spring." The curator responds, "Great, what's the exhibit about?" "Hmm," says the director, "I'm not sure yet. Why don't you just try out some stuff and see how it works?"

How likely is it that the curator will put together a great exhibit in time for the spring season? Not very. He needs to know what the exhibit is about—what is the theme, the message, the uniting principle?

I have worked with clients who are floundering like this. Michael was a high-level executive in a tech firm. He worked long hours and was typically on the road three or more days a week. In addition to his demanding job, he was a competitive triathlete, a gourmet cook, and a published novelist. Living the dream, right? Michael had grown up in a family where the mantra was, "You're as good as the best and better than the rest." To him, that meant he had to excel at *everything*. Excellence is a great goal, but it doesn't tell you what the exhibit that is your life should be focused on.

That's why you have to start by figuring out what's important. The first step is *identifying your values*. Remember Kelly, my exhausted client? Kelly had pushed herself beyond her mind and body's limits and she was paying the price in pain, confusion, and general misery. "What a silly woman!" you may be thinking. But Kelly wasn't silly at all. She was smart, generous, and caring. She was hardworking and disciplined. She was trying her hardest to do her best—for others and for herself.

As Kelly and I talked about how she had come to this difficult place in her life, we began to explore her values. What were the qualities she respected most in herself and in others? Two values kept bubbling up. The first was persistence. Kelly had grown up in a family where people *never gave up*. Her immigrant parents had overcome huge obstacles to make a better life for their children. They both worked extremely hard at low-paying jobs so their children could go to university and succeed in their careers. Kelly had learned from an early age that "Quitters never win and winners never quit."

The second value was autonomy. It was very important to Kelly to be in charge of her own destiny. She did not like relying on others and hated asking for help. In fact, it was very difficult for Kelly to open up to me because she was intensely uncomfortable with sharing her distress and taking guidance from someone else.

Both persistence and autonomy are great values. Without them, people don't get much done because they give up easily and are overly dependent on others. The trouble is that we learn our fundamental values when we are young children. Little kids see the world in absolutes. Their rules are rigid and unchangeable. *Many of us as adults are still unconsciously living with values that are so harsh and uncompromising that they get in our way, rather than helping us be the best we can be.*

In order to make adult decisions about what really matters in our lives, we need to be clear about our values—both the adult, conscious ones that help us make good choices and the childish, unconscious ones that get in our way.

Many of you probably know about Sigmund Freud, the revolutionary psychiatrist in the late nineteenth and early twentieth centuries who created psychoanalysis. Freud was one of the primary advocates of the idea that the human mind has both conscious and unconscious elements. If you ever took a Psychology 101 course in college, you know about Freud's theory of the three parts of the mind:

- the id, where our voracious instinctual needs drive us to pursue instant and total gratification (unconscious)
- the super-ego, our internalized and extremely rigid self-judgments and expectations (unconscious)
- the ego, our conscious minds that strive to balance the hunger of the id, the rigidity of the superego, and the external realities of our lives.

For many years, Freud's theory had enormous influence, not only on psychology but on the general culture as well. But in the 1950s some psychologists started to challenge the whole concept of an unconscious mind. They argued that because there was no direct way to measure or observe unconscious processes, Freud's model was not useful as a scientific theory. They were right. At that time the only way to measure brain activity was by opening up someone's skull and applying electrical stimulation directly to their brain. Not surprisingly, very few people were willing to be subjects for such experimentation. As a result, by the time I went to graduate school in the 1970s, the Freudian approach had fallen out of favor in many psychology departments and institutions.

But then a remarkable thing happened. Over the next couple of decades new imaging techniques were developed that enabled scientists to observe the brain in action without opening up someone's head. Since the 1990s, fMRIs and other brain-imaging techniques have led to amazing advances in our understanding of how the brain works.

Guess what! It turns out that in many ways, Freud was right. (Not about everything. Very few women would agree with his notion that our joy at having a baby boy is because he provides us with the male anatomy we lack and long for. As the mother of three boys, I can assure you that is nonsense. But that's a topic for another book.) Modern brain research has revealed that there are indeed two different and parallel processing modes in the human brain, one conscious and one unconscious. There is ongoing work being done to map and understand how these processes work.[1]

In the meantime, while the scientists explore this stuff, the rest of us have to figure out what's going on in our conscious and unconscious minds and use that information to curate our lives.

Identifying your values has two steps. First, you have to identify your *conscious* values. Here's an example of a client who engaged in that exploration. Zeke was a brilliant young rabbi. He had been a superstar at the seminary and everyone predicted that he would have an outstanding career. Zeke told me that in the rabbinic world the most prestigious jobs were highly paid pulpits in major urban congregations. These are demanding jobs, but they offer the possibility of having broad impact. These rabbis can influence not only the members of their congregation but also the wider community. They can have a political and economic impact as well as fulfilling their roles as spiritual leaders, teachers, and moral exemplars.

But within the Jewish community there was another rabbinic trajectory. Younger rabbis were exploring new congregational models and seeking new paths to reach out to Jews who were not affiliated with formal Jewish institutions. Zeke was drawn to the energy and creativity that he saw among these rabbis.

He had been offered both kinds of opportunities and he was struggling to decide. What was the best use of his talents and abilities? Where would he find the most joy and fulfillment? Which path would enable him to have a more curated life? What did God want him to do?

Zeke was fortunate because his strong religious commitment and deep education had given him the tools to make these kinds of moral choices, and he chose the path that he saw was right for him. Many people struggle with these kinds of choices without the tools that Zeke was able to deploy.

Nonetheless, if you are a reflective, self-aware person, you can probably sit down and make a list of your values pretty easily. My friend and colleague Dr. John Blattner taught me three questions to ask myself about my work:

- Am I doing good work?
- Am I having fun?
- Am I making money?

I love those questions, and I have used them many times in assessing both my own work situation and my clients' lives. Let's unpack the values that underlie the questions.

Am I doing good work? That taps into values such as excellence, achievement, having an impact, making a contribution, and being accountable.

Am I having fun? That reflects values such as joy, freedom, humor, and playfulness.

Am I making money? That connects into values such as financial security, being the best, responsibility, and fairness.

Maybe Dr. Blattner's questions resonate for you. Or perhaps you prefer the outline my client Anne gave me. Her most important values are beauty, success, holiness, and joy. Anne is someone who beautifies everything around her. She is a sensual person, and it matters to her how things look, sound, feel, taste, and smell. She is an ambitious person who wants to be known, respected, and well compensated. Anne is deeply religious and constantly measures her behavior against the standards and expectations of her religious tradition. And she believes that God wants people to be joyful and savor the delights and pleasures that the world has to offer.

My friend Rana Komar says that when it comes to work, people should ask themselves, "Will this bring me fame, fortune, or fun?" If you're getting all three, fantastic! But if one or more of these is missing, you need to think about how important that reward is for you. For example, if all you're getting is a big, fat paycheck and you're not having much fun, that may not work for you. If you're not answering yes to any of the three, find something else to do!

Sigmund Freud suggested that a productive and meaningful life rested on two values: love and work. There are many approaches to help you think about what matters to you.

Some people suggest that the best way to assess your values is to look at how you manage your money. How much goes to food? Alcohol? Travel? Education? How much are you saving for the future? How much do you give to worthwhile causes? What do your spending habits tell you about what is most important to you?

Another suggestion is to look at your calendar to find out what really matters to you. But I don't find this one so helpful. The reason for this book is that for so many of us, our calendars *don't* reflect our values. We spend a lot of time on low-value activities that are neither productive, meaningful, nor joyful for us and the people around us. In fact, if your calendar reflects your values, I would say you are already living a well-curated life.

Besides informal self-assessment, there are more formal tools you can use to help you get clear on your values and priorities. If you Google "free values assessment" you'll find a whole bunch of available tools. As a psychologist, I have extensive training in statistics and test design and I know that many of those tools have not been rigorously developed. But for our purposes, that's not so critical. The goal is to stimulate your thinking and awareness about what really matters to you, and these simple tools can help with that.

I tried out one called The Personal Values Assessment (https://www.valuescentre.com/our-products/products-individuals/personal-values-assessment-pva). It takes five minutes to complete, and then you get a report back in a couple of minutes. My report seemed accurate and thoughtful. Of course, this is based on my self-description, so it tells me how I see myself, not how others see me. But again, for our purposes it can be useful.

Another online tool that was recommended to me is the Life Values Inventory (http://www.lifevaluesinventory.org/). I tried it out and liked it because it moves beyond assessment to suggestions for how to incorporate your values into your life.

At the back of *The Power of Full Engagement* in the Resources section there is a Vision Worksheet with some great questions to help you think about what's important to you.[2]

A carefully designed and researched alternative is the *Hogan Assessment*. The Hogan is widely used in American business to help leaders assess whether people are a good fit for a specific job or company. One part of the Hogan is the Motives, Values, Preferences Inventory (MVPI). The MVPI measures ten motives or values: recognition, power, hedonism, altruism, affiliation, tradition, security, commerce, aesthetics, and science. (I find some of these names a little funky, but the tool really does get at a wide spectrum of values and priorities.) After you take it, you will get feedback from a certified Hogan consultant. The process is not free. To learn more, go to their website http://www.hoganassessments.com.

This is by no means an exhaustive list of tools that can help you identify your values. Friends, teachers, consultants, and others are good sources for other instruments.

Another approach to identifying your values is to ask people who are close to you what they think your values are. This can be very enlightening, because they may not see you exactly as you see yourself. It can also be interesting to compare your actual lived values with the values you aspire to.

An example: James was a partner in a consulting firm. He worked very hard to achieve his leadership position. He valued loyalty, dedication, intelligence, and a fierce work ethic. James believed it was his responsibility as a leader to mentor younger workers and help them navigate their careers. He was proud of his ability to identify and develop the talents of the people who reported to him and described his style as "firm but fair." But if you asked the people who worked for James, they saw him as valuing power, money, and people who reminded him of himself. They were afraid of his biting criticism and his sudden disapproval. Where James saw himself as generous, others saw him as controlling and self-centered.

The problem is that the "Jameses" of this world rarely get useful feedback on how others see them. They persist in their distorted beliefs about themselves and the values they are living. Fortunately for James, his company utilized a 360° feedback process for senior leaders. For those of you who aren't familiar with 360s, they are a widely used evaluation technique in the business world. You receive feedback from a list of people including your boss, peers, and subordinates, as well as other stakeholders such as clients (hence the term "360"—the full circle around you). The feedback may be gathered in interviews and/or a survey. Each respondent's answers are strictly confidential. The person being evaluated receives a verbal and/or written summary of how others describe him or her—both strengths and weaknesses.

I first learned about 360° feedback when I was in business school, and I thought it was one of the scariest things I had ever heard of. But since then I've been through several 360s myself and have administered and interpreted hundreds of them for others. I have learned that it is one of the most powerful ways to learn about yourself—your impact, your behavior, and your lived values. In my experience, 360° feedback is a very useful tool for motivating leaders to change and grow.

That's what happened with James. He was shocked when he learned that people saw him as a tyrant who enjoyed hurting others' feelings. He reflected on his leadership style and learned to deliver feedback in a more respectful and considerate manner. When a second 360° feedback process was completed a year later, James was very relieved to learn that his leadership impact had become much more congruent with his values.

Whatever tools you use, it's important to start your life curation by getting clear about what is most important to you. This clarity will underlie and inform the rest of the work you do to create your curated life. Be sure to keep your list brief. A list of thirty-five values is not going to help you make choices. Instead, focus in on your top five.

Now might be a good time to take a break. You could look out the window, or even step outside and walk around the block. Give yourself some time to reflect on what you've been reading and then come back.

As I said, the search to identify your values has two parts: identifying your conscious values, which we've just explored, and identifying your *unconscious* values—those rules and beliefs, mostly from childhood, that hold huge power over us and the choices we make. Those are a lot tougher to identify. You'll find them in places where you are irrational—where you are making choices that don't work well for you. You'll find them in repetitive patterns, mistakes you make over and over again.

You'll find them in the voice of the "Obnoxious Roommate." You know him or her—that voice in your head who relentlessly points out and magnifies your flaws and shortcomings. He's the guy who's very happy to tell you what's wrong with you. She's the girl who explains why your good fortune is undeserved, or is going to lead to more problems for you.

Digging out those hidden, rigid values is hard work. You can do some of that work alone, but many people need to talk with a therapist to really get at some of that deeper stuff. There was a time when we thought therapy was just for "sick" people, but we know now that it is also a very powerful tool for well people who want to enhance their effectiveness and their happiness.[3]

Here's an example of how unconscious values can derail you. William was a brilliant researcher at a pharmaceutical company. He read constantly, talked with other scientists, and was extremely well-informed about his field. He had the ability to put data together in creative ways and come up with solutions and inventions that no one else had thought of. But his career stalled because he was constantly leaving his projects unfinished. When he got close to completion, he would lose interest and head off in a different direction. Often his projects were finished by others, and then they got the credit for the work he had done.

William was very frustrated by his lack of career progress, and he knew he was not living up to his potential. He had no idea why he was sabotaging himself. As we talked about his dilemma, he shared with me that he was the only survivor of a terrible fire that had killed his parents and younger sister. He and his sister had been playing with a candle, which tipped over and started the conflagration. He sat quietly for a long time and then said, "I have no right to be here. I should have died with the others."

In William's childish value system, the fire was not an accident. He had committed a crime that was punishable by death. And so he was committing career suicide—over and over again. He had to learn to forgive that little boy he had been, and then he was free to become the man he was capable of being.

Here's another approach. The famous performance coach Tony Robbins has developed an exercise he calls "The Dickens Process" (https://www.businessinsider.com/tim-ferriss-tony-robbins-exercise-2017-1). The idea comes from Charles Dickens's tale *A Christmas Carol*. In Dickens's book the villain, Ebenezer Scrooge, is transformed overnight by visions of three ghosts: Christmas Past, Christmas Present, and Christmas Yet to Come. The emotional impact of those three visions fundamentally changes how Scrooge sees himself and others and enables him to become a better man.

The Dickens technique is designed to trigger the same kind of transformative change. First, you must identify your "limiting beliefs"—ways of thinking and understanding the world that are holding you back from being as successful and fulfilled as possible. That's important work for all of us, but the Dickens Process takes the work to the next level.

In the Dickens Process, you must emotionally connect with the weight and the pain your limiting beliefs are causing you. That means traveling back into the past to feel how those beliefs have damaged you and those around you. It means facing what those beliefs are costing you in the present—financially, interpersonally, spiritually. And it means experiencing what your future will be like—five years from now, ten years from now—if you continue to hold those beliefs. The goal is to "see it, hear it, feel it."

Transformative change rarely happens on the basis of thinking alone. It requires powerful emotional honesty to energize us to do the hard work of improving ourselves. The Dickens Process is one way to accelerate that journey.

A word of warning, though. If you want to utilize the Dickens Process, I strongly recommend that you only do so with an experienced, qualified coach. This kind of exploration can trigger very powerful feelings, so you need a guide you respect and trust. As my father, an expert therapist, said, "Only spill your guts to someone when you are sure they know how to put them back in the right place."

How do you find a good coach? That's a tricky problem because anyone can call him- or herself a coach. There is no regulation, so people can call themselves "life coaches" when in fact they are wanna-be therapists who don't have the proper training. A good coach understands the differences between coaching and therapy. Coaching is about helping people tackle specific performance challenges, usually in their work lives. It is typically more directive than therapy. Good coaches do not tackle mental health issues—they refer their clients to therapists for those challenges.

You can find coaches online, through professional organizations, and through your personal network. If you are seeking a good coach, I recommend that you consider the following questions:

- What are this person's academic qualifications? Does he have a coaching certification from a legitimate coach training program? Does she have an advanced degree in psychology or a similar discipline?
- What is this person's professional experience? Has he been a coach for a long time? Does she have experience in your industry that enables her to understand your world?
- Is this person recommended by someone you trust?

- When you are with this coach, do you feel understood, challenged, and safe?

Most coaches will have an initial conversation with you for free. Take that opportunity to size up the coach and ask questions like the ones above. Pay attention to your gut—the fit between the coach and the client is one of the most important predictors of success.

Whether you work with a coach or on your own, discovering and challenging your rigid, childhood values is *liberating*. You'll get better at navigating the land mines that lie in your path. You will be more aware of your vulnerabilities and better able to protect yourself. You'll get smarter about detecting the manipulations of people who do not have your best interests at heart. You will stop beating yourself up so much and start treating yourself with the same kindness you offer to others. And you will be able to focus your energy on the activities that truly matter to you—the ones where you want to be great.

Once you have identified your values, both the conscious and the unconscious ones, your next challenge is to identify your activities. Your list of conscious values gives you information about what is most important to you. Your increased awareness of your unconscious values gives you insight into what may be holding you back. Now you need a list of activities—both the things you are currently putting your energy into and the things you would *like* to put your energy into.

Here is a list of the broad categories into which most of our activities fit:

- Work/looking for work
- Family—childcare, eldercare, time with your partner, family gatherings
- Fun—leisure activities, artistic and creative pursuits, goofing around
- Health—exercising, other health routines
- Self-care—meditation, prayer, relaxation, massage

- Community/religious involvement
- Cleaning/maintenance—household chores, auto maintenance, yardwork
- Personal finances and other paperwork
- Travel—include this under the reason for the travel, such as work, family, or fun
- Personal grooming
- Shopping—if you like shopping, some or all of this may go under fun
- Learning—formal schooling as well as informal learning
- Eating and drinking—preparation, consumption, cleanup
- Phone, mail, email, social media
- Other

Creating your values list and your activities list will help you sort out your priorities and begin the curation process. Here are some examples:

Jan places a high value on aesthetics. How things look really matters to her, including her office. She enjoys wandering through beautiful stores even when she doesn't buy anything. She gets satisfaction from buying just the right piece of art to fit her workspace and please her eye. By contrast, Amy values thrift and functionality. Fancy stores irritate her because all she thinks about is how people are wasting their money on stuff she finds frivolous. She wants her workspace to be utilitarian and couldn't care less about how it looks.

Jason places very high value on family. He's been married for three years and he really wants children. He likes his job, but his identity is much more tied up in his personal relationships than in what he does for a living. Rob is an actor. He is passionate about his art and thinks of little else. Between taking auditions, performing, and getting ongoing coaching in acting, dance, and singing, he has little time for socializing, let alone relationships.

AJ believes that God put him on earth to make the world a better place. He needs to feel that his work matters, that it is making a difference to people in need. He is willing to put in long hours in difficult working conditions in order to fulfill his sense of purpose. On the other hand, Melissa wants financial security. In fact, she wants to be rich. She grew up in poverty and never wants to be there again. She looks forward to using her money for good purposes someday, but right now she just wants to build her fortune. She is willing to put in long hours in difficult working conditions as long as she is paid a boatload of money.

These are all pretty obvious examples of how people's values inform the choices they make about how they spend their energy. There are three key points they illustrate:

- *To maximize your productivity and happiness, you need to know what your values are and then focus your energy on the activities most congruent with those values.* The better you are at doing that, the more authentic and genuine you will feel and the more productive you will be.
- *There is not one right answer.* Jan will be happy spending more time shopping than Amy does. Jason should start planning a family but this is not the right time for Rob. AJ and Melissa may both make big contributions to the world, but they will do it in very different ways.
- *The process of curation changes over time.* This is not a one-and-done. We'll spend more time on that in chapter 9.

My guess is that right now the way you are apportioning your energy is not a perfect fit with your value system. You are probably spending way too much time doing stuff that feels unimportant and dumb and not enough on the things that really matter to you. Your curation is out of whack, and as a result the exhibit that is your life doesn't look so pretty to you.

In order to have a more beautifully curated life, you will have to learn to do three things:

1. *Say no.* Identify the things you are *just not going to do*—at least, not right now. Then take the steps to *eliminate* those activities from your life.

2. *Be mediocre* . Many people have the belief, "If you can't do something really well, then don't do it at all." Baloney! That is one of those unhelpful, rigid values we need to outgrow. The truth is that *most of what we do, we do so-so*. No one is great at everything they do. In fact, people who are really outstanding usually do *just one thing* . Figure out what you will be mediocre at and give those activities only as much energy as they absolutely require.

3. *Be great*. The well-lived life includes some thing or things you are really passionate about, the things you want to be remembered for. Know what those things are and put your best energy into them.

These steps are not sequential, they are simultaneous. Together, they will enable you to lead your best life. I'll talk about each of them in much more detail in the coming chapters.

I recently heard a beautiful story from Rabbi David Russo that helps to visualize the process of curation:

> One day, a teacher entered her classroom and placed a glass jar on the table. She placed two large rocks into the jar until no more could fit. She asked the class if the jar was full and they all said, "Yes." She responded, "Really?" She pulled out a pile of small pebbles, added them to the jar, and shook it slightly until they filled the spaces between the rocks. Then she asked again, "Is the jar full?" The students agreed that it was. Next she added a scoop of sand to the jar. She filled the space between the pebbles and asked the question again. This time, the class was divided: some felt that the jar was obviously full, while others were wary of another trick. So she grabbed a pitcher of water and filled the jar to the brim, saying, "If this jar is your life, what does this experiment show you?" She continued, "The rocks represent the BIG things in your life—what you will value at the end of your life. The pebbles are the other things in your life that give it meaning. The sand and water represent the 'small stuff' that fills our time. Now think about

this: what would happen if I started with the sand or the peb-
bles?"

That's the problem—most of us have too much sand in our jars
and not enough room for the big rocks. So let's talk about how to
get some of that sand out of the jar. Or in the language of curation,
how to eliminate from our exhibit the items that really don't be-
long there.

KEY TAKEAWAYS

- In order to make adult decisions about what really matters in
  your life, get clear about your values—both the adult, conscious
  ones that help you make good choices and the childish, unconscious ones that get in your way.
- Once you have identified your top values, focus your energy on
  the activities most congruent with those values. The better you
  are at doing that, the more authentic and genuine you will feel.
- There is not one right answer.
- The process of curation changes over time. This is not a one-
  and-done.
- In order to have a more beautifully curated life, you need to
  learn to do three things:

  - Say no to the unimportant things.
  - Be mediocre at the medium-important things.
  - Be great at the truly important things. Know what those
    things are and put your best energy into them.

3

SAY NO

I am one of those people who keep a "to-do list." In the old days it was a paper-and-pencil list; now it is my task list in Outlook. Every task has a deadline date assigned to it. Each morning when I sit down at my desk, I review my list for that day. I check things off as I get them done. I like checking things off—it's very satisfying. At the end of the day I see what I haven't done and I assign it a new date. I am fully expecting that I will die with a to-do list.

There is always too much to do. So how do you ensure that you spend your energy on the things that matter? *You eliminate the things that don't.*

This is really not easy. Look, you have already eliminated the obvious stuff. I doubt you spend much time routinely reading newspapers from three months ago or measuring the height of the grass in your neighbor's yard or clipping out recipes that are written in Klingon.

The real challenge is eliminating good stuff—stuff you think is worthwhile or you like to do. It's like the poor art curator who has to decide whether to cut out the Renoir or the Degas from the art exhibit. One of them has to go.

(By the way, watch out for that feeling I described in the first paragraph—the joy of checking things off your list. That feeling can be misleading. It can get you to do ten little, unimportant tasks rather than focusing on the one really big and important one.)

Here are some questions to help you identify the activities it is time to eliminate.

- Is this important to me? On a scale of 1–10, how much does this matter to me?
- Is this important to others I care about or are influential in my life (like my boss)?
- What will happen if I don't do this?
- Does this make me happy? On a scale of 1–10, how happy?

If you like, you can make a little chart like in figure 3.1. Start with the lower left cell as a good place to find the stuff you can eliminate.

Here's a trick to use with your to-do list. Watch for the items you have postponed again and again. When that happens, one of two things is going on. One, the task is something important that you really don't want to do—like schedule your colonoscopy or have a difficult conversation with someone you care about. In that case, you're going to have to figuratively kick your own butt and make yourself do it ASAP. Or two, the task is something you think you *should* do but it really isn't very important to you. For me, that's stuff like figuring out all the benefits from my Amazon Prime account or cleaning out my basement file cabinet. These seem like a good idea, but the truth is—they really don't matter that much to me. So I keep postponing them. In that case, take the task off your list, because you're not going to do it, at least not right now. So why keep bothering yourself about it?

Years ago when I had three small children, I gave a presentation on work-life balance. (I don't use that term any more, but I did in those days.) As part of the presentation, I shared a list of the stuff I was no longer doing since I started having children. The list included:

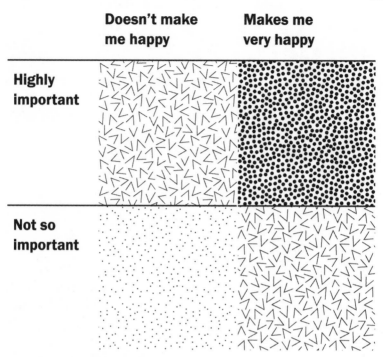

Figure 3.1.   Deciding what to eliminate. *Mary Clare Butler*

- going to professional conferences
- writing scholarly articles
- reading multiple professional journals and all the latest books
- serving on a community board
- sending holiday cards
- sewing my clothes
- hosting big parties
- reading novels
- doing our laundry
- baking bread
- a bunch of other stuff

Please note—all the things on the list were good things to do. Most of them were things I enjoyed (the laundry, not so much).

But in order to do the things that were really important to me—looking after my children, loving my husband, running a busy psychological practice—I had to cut all that stuff out. Most of the things on the list I have since reclaimed. Not the holiday cards or the sewing—they're gone forever.

Of course, I'm not suggesting your list should be the same as mine. But you do need to consciously decide what you're going to cut out—and then make it happen.

Be prepared—you will have to deal with three big problems. The first one is your own self-esteem. There's that voice in your head who says, "How can I be the kind of person who doesn't _____ (you fill in the blank)? Everyone else manages to get that done—why can't I?" That's the Obnoxious Roommate in your head talking, and we'll explore ways to quiet him or her down.

The second big problem is the reactions of others in your life. *People will judge you.* In some cases, they will be people who really don't matter to you, but sometimes they will be people who are important to you. People don't like it when you say "no" to them. We'll talk about navigating that challenge as well.

The third big problem is that sometimes saying no will make you sad. You may be letting go of an activity that used to matter to you or a dream you cared about. Perhaps a relationship has gone sour and it's time to let it go. We'll talk about how to navigate that sadness.

How do you stop doing activities that are not important enough for you to spend your energy on them? *One of the easier ways to eliminate activities is to delegate them.* Is there someone else who can do this task for you? Can you afford to pay someone to do it? This path feels good because even though you are no longer doing the task, it is still getting done.

In fact, delegation is not so easy. You have to find someone to whom you can delegate. That means assessing their availability, willingness, and skill to complete the task. At the beginning, you may have to train them to do the task, which can take *more* of your time than doing it yourself. Perhaps you can bring interns into your business to do some of the tasks that you are saying "no" to.

Perhaps you can delegate some of the housework to your children. But in both cases, you will have to teach and supervise until your assistants are ready to assume full responsibility for their tasks.

My colleague Nancy Picard has coached very senior executives. She taught me that business leaders need an "entourage." Think about movie stars—they usually have a whole staff of people who do tasks for them so they can focus on doing their creative work. One article lists the people a star needs in his/her entourage—the agent, the publicist, the mentor, the realist, and the cheerleader https://www.backstage.com/advice-for-actors/backstage-experts/5-people-every-actor-needs-their-entourage/. Many celebrities have much larger entourages, which include helpers like their house-keeper, lawyer, accountant, masseur, hair stylist, fashion stylist, trainer, and so on.

Few business leaders are going to have an entourage of that size or complexity. But according to Dr. Picard, in order to excel, business executives must create the entourage that enables them to perform at their peak, look polished in public, and maintain their health and well-being.

I think Dr. Picard is right—and I think even people who are not as much in the public eye need a smaller version of an entourage. Who is in your entourage? Make a list. There are probably some gaps. Keep this in mind as you keep navigating how to say "no." If you are paying members of your "entourage," you have to be comfortable that the value you gain from freeing up your time is worth the cost. One way to do that is to *calculate how much your time is worth.* That's relatively easy if you are in the paid work force. If your work is unpaid, there are resources to help you calculate the value of your time. For example, I googled "What is the annual value of a stay-at-home parent?" There are a bunch of websites that have ways to answer that question. A 2016 article from The National Association of Personal Financial Planners estimated the value of the work of a stay-at-home parent at about $140,000 annually (http://figuide.com/the-value-of-a-stay-at-home-parent.html). If you figure he or she works about 90 hours a week, that works out to about $31/hour. So paying someone else to do some part of the work at a similar or lower rate might make sense.

One of the big challenges about delegation is that you may have to lower your standards. Other people, especially if they are un-paid, often have their own way of doing tasks that is not identical to your way. For example, ask many business executives about how their employees write reports or prepare PowerPoint presenta-tions and you will hear their frustration. The grammatical and spelling errors, the lack of clarity, the poor graphic design—execu-tives can see the shortcomings and know they could do it better. Ask many women how their partners load the dishwasher and you'll hear the same frustration.

I employ other consultants in my business and they write re-ports on the clients they see. Those reports are on my letterhead and reflect my company's brand. When I first started reviewing others' reports, I found myself doing extensive rewriting. I wasn't managing my energy well, and I really wasn't making the reports better. My colleagues had different writing styles from me, but there wasn't anything really wrong with their style. I learned to back off and make comments only on really substantive issues.

Successful delegation requires that you don't hover over your helpers and micro-manage their activities. If you do, you won't save any of your energy, you'll annoy them, and they may just quit, or at least stop trying to do their best. That doesn't mean you can't have any standards at all. But remember, these are the activities that you have decided are relatively unimportant for you at this time in your life. So learn to let go.

Here's a work example. My client Christopher was the Chief Marketing Officer of a global consumer packaged goods company. He was a brilliant marketer who created innovative strategies and led his team to produce top-quality work. Unfortunately, he was widely disliked because of his excessive attention to detail. He insisted on editing minute details of others' work, such as the size of the graphics on a PowerPoint presentation. Unfortunately, my work with Christopher was not a striking success. He made a little progress in stepping back and letting others do their work, but he continued to insert himself all over the place where his attention was not needed. The result? He had less energy to do the big-picture work he was so talented at, and the morale on his team really suffered.

And here's a home example. One evening some years ago I was in my kitchen scouring the broiler pan after cooking dinner for my family. *I hate scouring broiler pans.* It's hard work and it's stinky and greasy. I thought to myself, "I am Dr. Golden, a highly re-spected and successful psychologist. I do not want to spend my time scouring broiler pans." So I said to my husband and kids, "I am done scouring the broiler pan. From now on, one of you has to do it."

I would be delighted to tell you that from that day on the men in my life gladly and conscientiously scoured the broiler pan. But that would be a lie. What I had to do was *leave the dirty broiler pan.* Sometimes it sat on the kitchen counter for days. But sooner or later someone would recognize that it needed to be done and the pan would be cleaned. To this day, I do not scour a broiler pan unless everyone else in the household is away on a long vacation.

(By the way, I am not suggesting that you have to be a highly educated professional in order to delegate work to other family members. That self-perception helped me to leave the task to others. But we all work hard at the tasks of our lives. So everyone has not just the right but actually the responsibility to delegate tasks and then let others do them in their own way.)

Psychologists have done research on the impact of microman-agers. For example, one study showed that the inability to delegate work to others has negative health consequences for the managers and increases their stress. It may also lead to diminished work performance.[1]

So learning to delegate, both at work and at home, is a crucial curation skill.

I want to mention that of course there is another delegation alternative. Besides delegating to people, we have increasing op-portunities to delegate to technology. Whether it's using a Room-ba to do your vacuuming or employing the latest high-powered people analytics tools to make your hiring processes more efficient, technology can simplify our lives in many ways. There are two important keys to this. First, you need to be open to new ways of doing things. Much as I love an old-fashioned dial telephone, I have to admit that my iPhone is a vastly more useful and efficient tool. The rapid pace of technological change makes it difficult to stay open to the new. Just when you've mastered a technological tool, it becomes obsolete and you have to learn the next one. But the benefits in enabling you to use your energy for the things you are uniquely capable of doing—they make it worth the trouble.

The second key is making sure that you are running the technology—it's not running you. Many people are feeling overwhelmed by the *demands* that technology places on them. I particularly loathe the self-checkout lines in grocery stores. Whether you're trying to navigate poorly designed websites or suffering from FOMO (Fear of Missing Out) that forces you to check social media every seventeen seconds, you're letting technology boss you around. That's not delegation—that's slavery!

Delegation is a good solution when it's possible. But sometimes there really isn't someone else who can do the job. If you say no, then the task will not get done. At that point, you have to ask yourself, "So what? If this task never gets done again by me or anyone else, so what?"

If saying no to the activity leads to dire consequences, then you have to reconsider your curation decision. But so often, if you stop doing some of these relatively low-value tasks, nothing much will happen. Remember my two activities that ended permanently when I had kids—sewing my own clothes and sending holiday cards? What do you think happened as a result? I had to spend a little more money to buy clothes. And I communicated less often with some of my distant friends. Neither of those consequences was disastrous. And the energy I saved by not doing those activities went into tasks I valued much more, such as spending time with my kids and staying up-to-date with research in my field.

So how do you deal with the guilt? With that voice that tells you how inadequate you are? You learn to talk back to the "Obnoxious

Roommate." Remember, that voice comes from your early child-hood, when you internalized rigid rules in a simplistic manner. So, answer back from your adult self.

- Would I talk to anyone else this way? If my friend was making the choices I am making, would I tell him how awful he is?
- What is the alternative? If I try to do everything, then I'll do nothing very well. I have to make choices, and this is what I choose.
- What is the ROI (return on investment)? How much will it cost me, in energy and money, to do this activity and what is the benefit I will derive?
- Laugh at yourself and your shortcomings. It doesn't have to be so grim and serious.

With practice, you can learn to quiet the Obnoxious Roommate. But out there in the real world, there are other people who may disagree with your decision to say no. They may disapprove of your choices out of their value system that says how people should be. They may be personally hurt that you aren't going along with what they want. Or both.

This leads us into another area for self-reflection. You need to ask yourself, *"How important is this person's opinion to me?"* I was on the bus a while back when a fellow passenger was very aggressively rude to me. I didn't want to inflame her further, so I responded in a quiet, pacifying manner and she settled down. When she got off the bus, I was congratulating myself for my mature handling of a difficult encounter. And then another passenger on the bus started to criticize me. Why hadn't I stood up for myself? Why had I let her push me around?

I must admit that I thought, "What is this, Beat Up on Gail Day?" But the point is, the guy who was criticizing me was a stranger, and I really didn't give a fig what he thought of me. In retrospect, it seemed almost funny that he felt the need to instruct me on how I should have comported myself. I certainly didn't feel guilty or inadequate about the choice I had made.

But—some of us really have difficulty with criticism from *anyone*. We want to please everyone all the time. We want everyone to like us and think we are wonderful all the time. Everyone's opinion matters to us, and this makes us terribly vulnerable.

Here's the thing about criticism (or feedback, as we sometimes call it). Sometimes it tells you more about the person who is giving the criticism than it does about you. Sometimes people are having a bad day, or you managed to push a button you didn't know was there, or they really don't know what they're talking about, or it's none of their business anyway.

If you are someone who has to please everyone all the time, remember where that comes from. That's one of those rigid rules you absorbed from early childhood. It's an impossible standard and it leads to misery. So once again, your task is to move into your adult self and learn to view criticism and judgment in a more reasoned way.

The most difficult challenge is when you have to say no to someone who really matters to you—a partner, a parent, a boss. You *do* care about their opinion, and sometimes you will change your mind based on their reaction. But sometimes you know your decision is the right one for you at this time, and you need to stand your ground.

Back in the olden days when I was young, there was a big fad called assertiveness training. The core idea was that you could respond to someone else in one of three ways:

- Passivity: You just go along with everything others want and you're pretty much a doormat.
- Aggression: You fight with people, you're rude and intimidating, but no one can boss you around.
- Assertiveness: You stand your ground and defend yourself without attacking others.

Guess which one was the recommended approach? Actually, each of the three kinds of behavior is the best choice in certain situations. If you're alone on the street at night and someone tells you to give him your wallet or he'll shoot you, most police officers will advise you to be passive and do what he tells you. If you're on the job and a fellow worker is making inappropriate sexual remarks to you, an aggressive response may get him to back off and leave you alone. But in most circumstances, especially when you want to maintain a positive, long-term relationship with the other person, assertiveness is the best choice.

Although assertiveness training fell out of fashion a long time ago, some of the key ideas are still useful. A couple of classic assertiveness tactics can be helpful when someone is questioning or criticizing your decision to say no. One tactic is "Fogging," which means that you find areas of agreement with the other person without changing your decision. Here's an example:

Your colleague: I can't believe you're taking off for vacation at such a busy time. You're leaving the rest of us to carry the load.

You: Yes, it's really busy right now. I'll do as much as I can before I leave.

Colleague: Well, it must be nice for you. You should have thought ahead before you planned to go at this time.

You: Yes, if I had known there would be such a crunch, I would have made a different plan.

Colleague: Well, I guess it's probably too late for you to change your plans.

Another tactic is "Broken Record," which means calmly repeating your point of view.

You: I've decided we're not coming to the family cottage this year. The kids and I are going to visit New York instead.

Your sister: What do you mean you're not coming? It's been our family tradition forever!

You: Well, we won't be coming this year. We really want to spend some time exploring New York.

Your sister: It won't be the same without you. Can't you change your mind?

You: We'll miss you, too, but this year we're going to New York.

If you are interested in learning more about assertiveness, check out these websites: https://www.betterhealth.vic.gov.au/health/ ten-tips/10-tips-for-being-assertive; https://www.artofmanliness. com/2013/02/12/how-to-be-assertive/. Or read one of the classic books about assertiveness, such as *When I Say No, I Feel Guilty*.[2]

Break time. Get up from your chair, take a few deep breaths, look out the window. Go have a chat with someone. Have a drink of water. See you in five to ten minutes.

In general, if you know you need to have a difficult or stressful conversation it's a good idea to practice in advance. Effective practice has several steps. Let's imagine your colleague, Jamal, wants you to help him plan an offsite for the leadership team. You are already spread way too thin at work, and you know that you would not be able to put in the energy that the project requires. Even though you like Jamal and are interested in the project, you just cannot wedge it into your schedule right now. How are you going to discuss this with Jamal?

First, think about what your goal is. When you walk away from the conversation, what will make you feel it was a success? For example:

- After I talk with Jamal, he will know I am not going to work on the offsite with him and he won't ask me again.
- I will still have a friendly, respectful relationship with Jamal.

- Jamal will keep me in mind for other projects in the future.

Second, think about the other person. If you were in his shoes, what would help you hear the message clearly? Directness is important, not some wishy-washy, "Well, let me think about it" and then you never get back to him. Regret might be helpful, showing that you understand that you are disappointing him. Appreciation for the offer opens the door to future possibilities.

Third, don't over-explain and over-apologize. Women are especially susceptible to this mistake, and it makes you vulnerable to manipulation by the other person. "Jamal, I'm so, so sorry, it's just that I have to have an unpleasant, embarrassing medical procedure, and my gambling debts have mounted up so I have to take a second job, and I have to visit my son who's in jail on a drug charge and it's 150 miles from here, and I feel so bad that I'm letting you down so maybe I could do some piece of the work after all." OK, I'm being a little sarcastic now, but I've heard people offer up these kinds of excuses. Doing so may salve your guilt a little, but it's demeaning to you and probably uncomfortable for the other person.

I usually have to work through several drafts in my mind before I come up with a conversational script that works for me.

Version 1: Forget it, Jamal, I'm not interested in the offsite so back off and don't ask me again. (Too aggressive, in case you didn't figure that out for yourself)

Version 2: Oh, Jamal, I'd really, really like to help with the offsite, but I don't know, I've got a lot going on at the moment. (Too vague)

Version 3: Uh, Jamal, I didn't have time to think about it yet. I'll get back to you. (Too passive-aggressive)

Version 4: Hey, Jamal, I'm sorry but I won't be able to work with you on the offsite. It sounds like a great project, but I just don't have the bandwidth right now. I hope we'll have a chance to work on something else together in the future. (Not bad—direct, regretful, appreciative)

The challenge is to find your own voice that is firm, clear, and unequivocal. Keep working on your message until you feel comfortable delivering it. But there's still another problem. Jamal is going to respond, and unfortunately you don't get to write his lines for him. So, you need to think about his probable responses and how you will deal with them.

Scenario 1:

Jamal: Oh, man, you are really leaving me in a bad spot. I was counting on you. Come on, there's gotta be a way you can help me out.

You: Yeah, I'm sorry, but I just can't. I hope you'll be able to find someone else. (Broken Record, empathy, not owning what is really his problem)

Scenario 2:

Jamal: Oh, I know, it's always like this. Jamal has to be the one to do the work because everyone else is "too busy." (Guilt trip)

You: Yeah, you have a tough job. (empathy but not falling into the guilt trap)

Scenario 3:

Jamal: What's so important that you can't help me out? (Nosy Parker. Watch out—this is a trap.)

You: I just don't have the bandwidth right now. I hope we'll have a chance to work together on something else. (Broken Record, no detailed explanations)

Scenario 4:

Jamal: Well, the hell with you. You wouldn't have been any use anyway. (Aggressive, blaming)

You: Hey, good luck on the project. (Not engaging, ending the conversation)

Scenario 5:

Jamal: Shoot, that's too bad. I really was hoping we could work together. (Whew, that's what I wanted to hear.)

You: Yeah, me too. I'm sure there will be other opportunities down the road. (Mission accomplished, hurray!)

It's also important to think about which communication medium you will use to say no. Figure 3.2 provides a good guideline.

Email, texting, and similar communication channels are extremely treacherous and should almost never be used for a high-intensity communication. There are three main reasons why they are so dangerous. First, it is very hard for the other person to read your tone. Email often comes across much harsher than you intend. Even with low-intensity emails, I usually use an "email sandwich." It looks like this:

> Hi, Trey—hope you're having a good day and the ABC project is doing well. I won't have time to read the draft you sent me until next week—I'm just swamped. I'll get it to you by end of day on Monday. Give my best to Kiara, hope to see you guys soon. All the best, Gail

The first part of the email sandwich is the top slice of bread, "Hope you're having a good day. . . ." Then comes the filling, which is the real message. The last sentence is the bottom slice, "Give my best to Kiara. . . ."

OK, you may be thinking this is dumb and a waste of time. But now read the email without the sandwich:

> I won't have time to read the draft you sent me until next week—I'm just swamped. I'll get it to you by end of day on Monday.

Level of emotional complication/likelihood of misunderstanding	Best communication medium
Low	Email Text Phone call Videochat In-person
Medium	Phone call Videochat In-person
High	In-person if at all possible Videochat
Medium or High with a need for a permanent record	Videochat, phone call or in-person followed by a written document or recording

Figure 3.2.   Choosing a communication channel. *Mary Clare Butler*

If you and Trey have a great relationship, that might work. But it comes across kind of high-handed and brusque. Trey can't hear your tone of voice or see your face to know that you're truly regretful. So, most of the time, you need to use the sandwich.

What about emoticons? Most people agree they are too informal for business communication. The one exception is ☺, which can be used to indicate that you are being funny. But I'd recommend using it very sparingly.

So, to recap, the first problem with email is that your reader can't sense your emotional tone. The second problem is that you won't see the impact of your email. That makes it really easy to send nasty, harsh emails, especially when you're ticked off. People say things in emails they would never say to a person's face. It's pretty easy to drop a bomb when you don't see the devastation below.

The third problem with email is that it's too easy to send. In the old days, if you wanted to send a nastygram you had to type or write a letter, sign it, put it in an envelope, put a stamp on it, and take it to the mailbox. By that time, you might well have decided that you should rethink the message you are sending. With email, you can write that sucker and hit send before your blood has stopped boiling.

The best advice is—don't use email to deal with emotionally complicated situations. If you are feeling afraid, or angry, or very sad, email is probably not your best choice. If email is your only channel, then write a draft and save it. Don't send it until your emotions have settled down and you can review it and make a reasonable decision about whether to go ahead. Double-check to be sure there's no unwanted "tail" of previous emails that you don't want to be sharing. And be careful not to hit "send" by accident. (Here's a tip from my son, Aaron—don't put the recipient's email address in until you're sure you want to send it.) In many cases you will feel somewhat calmer after you have written the draft and you'll decide to edit it before you send it, or not send it at all.

You may think I am making too big a deal about email. But I have seen a whole bunch of executives who got into trouble for sending an impulsive, ill-considered email. Those emails can derail your career. So heed my advice—be thoughtful before you hit "send."

The phone is much better than email, because it gives both parties information about each other's emotional nuances. It also puts you into communication at the same moment and makes it easier to sort out misunderstandings right then. Videochat is one step better because you get some of the nonverbal cues that make it easier to read each other. Best of all is the face-to-face conversation because it facilitates real empathy and understanding.

Some of you may be thinking that I'm an old fuddy-duddy for my emphasis on phone calls and in-person meetings to deal with complicated situations. It's true—I didn't grow up with the communication options that we have now. But I have talked with many "digital natives" and they consistently agree with me—the best human connections are made in person.

One final note about communication channels. In my chart I mentioned the need to create a written document or recording of some conversations. There is huge value in such documentation. Early in my career I rented a room in the home of another woman who worked in the same company as me. When I moved in, we talked about how we would split the cost of the utilities. It was a large house, so we agreed I would pay 25 percent of the cost. But when the bills came in, her recollection was different and she insisted that I pay 50 percent of the bills. I had no recourse—it was her house and I had no record of our conversation. I resented her, but there was nothing I could do. If we had just written our agreement down and both signed it, we could have prevented the bad feelings.

Whether it's a contract of some kind or a meeting in which people commit to certain tasks, a written record can prevent a lot of frustration. When I am coaching someone and they're not writing anything down, I'm pretty sure they aren't going to follow through on what we're talking about.

We've been talking about the skills of saying no—being clear about your objectives, considering the other person's perspectives, practicing in advance, and using the right communication channel. You need all of these skills to handle one of the most challenging "say no" situations—limiting or moving out of "energy drain" relationships. These are out-of-balance relationships, where the energy you put in is much greater than the energy you get out of the relationship.

I am not suggesting that people should always keep a transactional account of the give-and-get in relationships. If you are a caring and connected human being, you will be in some give-more-than-you-get, energy-drain relationships. For starters, a relationship between an adult and a baby or a young child is *always* an energy-drain relationship. Similarly, caring for an ill friend or family member is likely to be an energy-drain. We choose these relationships because we love the people or we feel an obligation to help someone who needs our assistance—and good for us!

But there are other energy-drain relationships that are imposed on us. In your family there may be people who are manipulative, needy, and demanding, or angry, bossy, and demeaning. As they say, you don't get to choose your relatives.

In the workplace this is also a huge issue. When I coach people who are unhappy at work, in many cases they are working with energy-drain colleagues. These colleagues may be people who are sad and pathetic and you feel as if you should be taking care of them. They may be people who are passive-aggressive, undermining the progress of your work and frustrating you. They may be bosses who are nit-picky micromanagers. I'm sure you have no trouble identifying these folks in your workplace. They're the ones you're lying awake stewing about at 3 a.m.

How do you say no to these people—or at least limit their impact on you? Sometimes you have to end the relationship—request a transfer, leave the job, get a divorce. But often that's not possible or desirable. So one option is to limit your contact with the person.

When Paige was a university student, there was a woman in her program, Angela, who was quite depressed. She would often come and stand in the door of Paige's office, not saying anything. Even though Paige was under great pressure to get her work done, when she saw Angela, she felt obligated to ask her in—and then they would have a long, time-consuming conversation about all Angela's troubles. Paige found she was beginning to duck and hide when she saw Angela coming. But that's what most people were doing, and it just made Angela unhappier. So instead, one day

Paige said, "Look, I'm busy right now and I can't talk. How about if we go out for lunch once a week, starting on Thursday?" Angela looked surprised but agreed, and after that they went for lunch regularly. Two things happened. First, Angela stopped standing in Paige's doorway. And second, to Paige's great surprise the lunches turned out to be quite pleasant.

I like this solution because it is kind both to the other person and to yourself.

Another way to reduce the impact of an energy-drain relationship is to make sure you're not letting the person inside your head. Remember the Obnoxious Roommate? Many energy-drain people are great at feeding that voice in your head that tells you everything that's wrong with you. So another way of saying no is to shut that voice up.

Andrew worked on a consulting team where the team leader, Marcie, really didn't like him. He never understood why, but he consistently got negative feedback from her, both directly and indirectly. She gave him make-work projects that wasted his time. He made numerous attempts to improve the relationship but was never successful. She was always superficially pleasant to his face, but the indirect messages and vibes were truly hostile. He began blaming himself for the problem and floundering around trying to find ways to make her like and respect him. Finally, he realized the solution lay in his own head. "I get to live the rest of my life being Andrew, and she is stuck being Marcie," he thought. And with that, her power over him was diminished. He continued to work with her as best he could, but he focused his energy elsewhere.

Saying no is an essential part of curating your life. It's a high-level complex task that requires negotiating both with yourself and with others. As I mentioned in chapter 1, when I started going to business school I was still working full-time as a psychologist and caring for my family. I sat down with my husband and my youngest son, who was still living at home, and we talked about how we would navigate this challenge together. Among other things, my husband agreed to take over all the cooking for the next two years, and he followed through on that commitment. He bought our first microwave and did a great job of keeping us fed and happy.

But sometimes saying no has painful consequences. The other big thing I cut out of my life during my years in business school was socializing with my friends. I told my friends, regretfully, that I was going to be pretty unavailable for the next two years and that I looked forward to reconnecting with them when I came up for air. Most of my friends were understanding and supportive. But I lost one friend. He was very angry and felt I was thoughtlessly discarding our relationship. I reached out to him after I graduated and never heard a word back. That was disappointing—but the curation was essential and it was a price I had to pay for focusing on what was most important to me at that time.

Saying no does not mean you think only about yourself and are callous toward others. But it also does not mean that you think only of others and fail to do what is right for you. You can be empathic to others' feelings and responsive to their needs while still being focused on what is most important to you. The famous Golden Rule (which I wish I had written but I didn't) is "You shall love your neighbor as yourself." It does *not* say, "You shall love your neighbor and not yourself." In fact, I would argue that the true meaning of the Golden Rule is that you can only love others to the extent that you love yourself.

Sometimes saying no is disappointing. You would really like to do the project you are turning down. Sometimes it's scary. You worry that you are wrecking an important relationship by saying no. And sometimes it's sad. Perhaps a relationship has gone sour. Perhaps a career you thought you would love has turned out to be miserable. The more energy you have invested in something, the more likely it is to be sad when you choose to say no. It can take real courage to make that choice. Be kind to yourself. Give yourself time to feel the sadness and then let it go.

Part of saying no is saying good-bye. That can be a relief, it can be liberating, but it can also be exhausting. When it was time for me to leave my clinical practice and become a consultant, it felt as if I spent more than three months doing nothing but saying good-bye to people. Not only was I saying good-bye to my therapy clients, but we were also moving to a different city, so I was saying good-bye to all my friends as well. There were innumerable conversations and social gatherings and professional events where I was saying good-bye. I remember the moment when I climbed into our car and set out for our new home, leaving my old life behind. My first thought was, "Thank goodness I am done for now with saying good-bye!"

To sum up, saying no can trigger all kinds of unpleasant emotions: guilt, loss, disappointment, and sadness, among others. So besides mastering the communication skills to say no kindly but firmly, we also have to learn how to recognize and manage our own emotional reactions. It's a complicated set of skills, which helps to explain why so many of us have so much difficulty saying no to the relatively unimportant, uninteresting, or low-value activities in our lives.

Warning: There are times when you should not say no. There are people who are saying no to too many things. Here are some examples of things you should generally not say no to:

- Taking care of your personal hygiene
- Feeding yourself in a healthy manner and engaging in other healthy behaviors
- Spending time with people who are good to you
- Engaging in activities you love
- Doing meaningful work

These are activities that are essential to a joyful and productive life. Saying no to some or all of them is often a symptom of depression. Depression is a serious psychological condition that saps your energy, your motivation, and your joy. If you are saying no too much—if you are limiting yourself to a narrow, unhappy life—then you should talk with your doctor about diagnosing and treating what is holding you back. For a simple checklist of symptoms of depression, see https://www.uclahealth.org/resnick/checklist-for-depression .

There is a saying, "If you want a job done, give it to a busy person." There's some truth to that. Busy people are usually good at what they do and also good at organizing what they do. But what if you are the busy person everyone else relies on to get the job done? You have to learn how to curate, and that means saying no sometimes.

Saying no is part of your personal power. It is a way of valuing yourself and demonstrating that value to others. It is a way of preventing others from taking advantage of you. You will never be the person you are capable of being if you can't say no. And remember, saying no may actually mean "not now." Some nos are forever, but many nos can be changed as you move on in your life.

One of my clients was a senior executive at a major financial institution. He taught me his motto, "Only do what only you can do." In my experience, that's aspirational. Everyone sometimes has to do things that could easily be done by others—take out the garbage, take minutes in a meeting, whatever. But his motto is useful. Am I focusing on the things that I am uniquely capable of doing or frittering away my energy on things that could be done just as well or better by others?

Only do what only you can do.

KEY TAKEAWAYS

- Ensure that you spend your energy on the things that matter by eliminating the things that don't.
- Ask yourself:

  - Is this important to me?
  - Is this important to others who matter to me?
  - What will happen if I don't do this?
  - Does this make me happy?

- Saying no is hard because:

- it can make you think less of yourself;
- other people will judge you;
- it may make you sad.

- One of the easier ways to eliminate activities is to delegate them.
- Sometimes you have to leave the dirty broiler pan.
- Deal with the negative voice in your head by responding:

  - Would I talk to anyone else this way?
  - What is the alternative?
  - What is the ROI?
  - This is actually kind of funny.

- Deal with criticism by asking, "How important is this person's opinion to me?"
- Handle difficult conversations by:

  - using assertiveness;
  - practicing in advance;
  - using the right communication channel (which is usually not email).

- Give yourself time to feel the sadness and then let it go.

4

EMBRACE MEDIOCRITY

Oh, that word "mediocre." It's such a tyrant. When I talk with people about curation, they often find it fairly easy to identify what they want to be really good at. What's harder is choosing what they'll say "no" to. But hardest of all is to honestly and consciously decide to be mediocre at something.

Why is this so difficult? Once again, I think it starts with lessons we learned as young children. Parents rarely say to their kids, "Oh, sweetie, it's just fine to be mediocre at _____ (fill in the blank)." We want our kids to have high standards and a strong work ethic. So we tell them some variation of, "Always do your best," or "Don't do something unless you can be great at it."

John's father was a wonderful parent. They were very close and John's father was John's inspiration and role model. When he came home from school after an exam, his father would ask him, "How did you do?" Since John was a very good student, he would usually respond with something like, "I got 97 out of 100." And his father would always say, "What happened to the other three points?"

He was being funny. John knew his father was proud of him and his academic achievements. But years later, as he looked back at his academic career, he could see that his father's words had a profound impact. John felt he had to get an "A" in *everything*—

gym, wood shop, everything. It didn't matter if he was interested in the subject, or if the teacher wasn't very good. *He had to get all A's.*

There's a good side to that. In my scale of values, academic success is very important. I measure my own and others' level of achievement in part by how well we did in school. In my mind, students should take their work seriously and strive to do their best.

But there were two problems with John's father's message. First, he was asking for *perfection*. And as we all know, perfection is elusive. There was humor in his comment, but behind much humor is a serious message. John knew his father believed in him—and he also knew his father wanted him to be perfect.

And there's the second problem. Notice I didn't say, "His father wanted him to be perfect *at his schoolwork*." That would be hard enough! But as a child, John generalized the message. In his mind, his dad wanted him to be perfect at *everything*.

My friends, that is a setup for failure. Even Leonardo da Vinci wasn't perfect at everything. With that mindset, you will live your entire life feeling not good enough. And you will waste your precious energy aiming for perfection in activities that really aren't that important.

Furthermore, we know that perfectionism in the workplace does *not* contribute to better outcomes. In fact, it has been linked to role stress, inefficiency, exhaustion, and cynicism.[1] The sad thing is that it's not just our remembered childhood messages that get in our way. The poison of perfectionism is in our current environment as well. How often have you heard someone say, "The good is the enemy of the great"? What? I know they mean you shouldn't settle for second-best. But they're flat wrong. The good is the *friend* of the great. By settling for good—or even mediocre—in some parts of your life, you free up your energy, creativity, and determination to become great at the really important activities.

You're not going to change the misguided people around you who tell you that you have to be great at everything. Nor can you change the childhood lessons you learned from very important and influential people in your life. The only thing you can change is you—right here, right now. You have to consciously and deliberately choose what you will be mediocre at.

Oooof! How do you do that? The process is actually quite similar to the sequence I outlined in the last chapter on saying "no." First, let's revisit the questions we started with there (with slight modifications and additions):

- Is this activity important to me? On a scale of 1 to 10, how much does this matter to me?
- Is this important to others I care about or are influential in my life (like my boss)?
- What will happen if I do this to a mediocre standard?
- Does this activity make me happy? On a scale of 1 to 10, how happy?
- Whose standards matter to me on this task? My own or someone else's?

Once again, one of the key considerations in choosing mediocrity is ROI. What will it cost to meet the perfection standard, and what is the benefit of doing so? We all know situations in which people spend an inordinate amount of time trying to move a work product from 95 percent perfect to 100 percent perfect. If that work product saves lives—let's say you're a brain surgeon—then the standard *has to* be perfection because the cost of failure is devastating. But if you're spending two hours getting an image perfectly sized and positioned on a PowerPoint slide, maybe the cost of your energy is too high for the benefit of visual impact?

On the other hand, sometimes it is *more* expensive to do something in a mediocre manner because you'll just have to redo it. How many times have you put a loaf of bread in the oven and wandered off to the other end of the house to do something else? And by the time you get back to the kitchen the bread is so overdone it's inedible? How many times have you submitted a complicated spreadsheet for an important meeting and then found it was riddled with errors? In both cases, your mediocre approach re-sulted in some combination of an unacceptable product, going hungry, being publicly humiliated, and/or having to redo the whole thing.

Choosing where to be mediocre is a deeply personal decision. For example, I am a fanatic about spelling, punctuation, and grammar. It drives me nuts when I read material by educated people and there are basic grammatical errors in it. It makes me think less of them. I always proofread my own work—even emails and texts—before I send it out, and it really bugs me when I find an error after I have submitted something. I know it is highly likely that somewhere in this book there are spelling or grammatical mistakes even though I have done my best to eliminate them. And it's really going to irritate me when I find them.

That doesn't mean everyone else has to be as nutty as I am about grammar. For me, it is part of my self-esteem and my brand that I use language correctly. But if it's not your thing, then mediocre grammar, at least some of the time, may be good enough for you.

And that's the key question—when is good enough good enough? For you and for others who are evaluating your work?

OK, let's assume you have identified some activities where it's good enough for you to be mediocre at them. My first piece of advice is you don't need to tell everyone about it. It's generally not their business anyway. Just quietly go about doing these tasks to your own mediocre standard. You will probably be surprised about *how few people actually notice.*

If you've been paying attention, you might now accuse me of being inconsistent. Because back in chapter 3, I warned you that people *are* going to judge you. That's true, and you do need to be prepared for criticism. But it is also true that we often imagine that others are paying a lot more attention to us than they actually are. People are busy with their own lives, they are trying to get their own work done, and much of the time they really aren't focusing on you or how well you're doing.

When Mariana entered graduate school, she was fortunate to be awarded a particularly generous package of financial assistance. Almost all the entering students received support of some kind, but most of them had to work for that support as research or teaching assistants. The grant Mariana received had both a higher stipend and no work requirement.

She was very grateful, but she also felt a little guilty that her fellow students had a tougher challenge than she did because of their extra workload. So she said to herself, "I got the cushier financial aid. That means I have to be the best on every single assignment, on every exam, in every course. Otherwise, the other students will resent me and feel I don't deserve the money I'm getting."

There were two big problems with that scenario. First, her fellow students were *really* smart. The program was very tough to get into and they were a highly select group. So the competition to be the best at everything all the time was going to be brutal. Second, the first-year program was designed to be a miserable experience for the students. They were required to take courses in all the areas of their field that were *not* their primary interest, taught by professors who put a higher priority on evaluating them than on teaching them.

So Mariana was setting an impossible standard for herself and adding to her own misery, all because she believed the other students were watching her grades very closely. It took her a semester to figure out that no one was paying the slightest attention to how well she was doing. Everyone was struggling to survive and cope with his or her own challenges.

Once she realized that no one else cared about her grades, she was able to take a breath, settle down, and just focus on doing the best she could at what mattered to her. As it turned out, she got excellent grades in graduate school, but not because she was trying to meet her imagined picture of others' impossible standards. She continued to be miserable in the program, so she decided the best approach was to get out as fast as she could. She worked out a three-year plan and ferociously stuck to it. In order to accomplish her goal, she had to get top grades so the faculty wouldn't try to slow her down. But honestly, she cut corners wherever she could. To put it another way, she accepted mediocrity in the service of speed. And it worked—she was out in three years with the credential she needed and she never looked back.

Here's another example of how people don't notice when you choose mediocrity. Stephanie was planning a big party and obsessing about every detail. She had hired a caterer, only to discover that the same caterer was preparing a friend's party only a week before hers. So she went to her friend, Naomi, and breathlessly said, "We better talk about the menus for our parties because otherwise we might be serving the same food." (Oh, no, what a disaster!) Naomi smiled at her and said, "Let me tell you a story. Several years ago I threw a big soiree. The food was great except for the carrots—they were just horrible. Several weeks later I met up with one of the guests and she talked about how much she had enjoyed the event. 'Yes,' I said, 'but wasn't it too bad about the carrots!' The guest looked surprised and said, 'What carrots?'"

What had seemed like such a big deal to Naomi was in fact utterly unimportant. Stephanie realized she was worrying way too much about a relatively minor part of the celebration. She relaxed, focused on how to give her guests a really great time, and the event went beautifully. Ever since then, when Stephanie finds she is freaking out about some detail, she asks herself, "Is this a 'carrot?'" Because if it is, it's not worth the energy it takes to worry about it.

So don't tell people about where you are choosing to be mediocre. And don't worry about who's judging you. No shame, no apologies. It's your life to make the most of. Just do it.

How about it? Time for a break? Listen to some music, get up and stretch, send a joke to a friend? Then come on back.

What are the activities where many people choose to set a mediocre standard? One is housekeeping. My personal opinion is if it's hidden, it's OK to be messy (inside closets, drawers, the refrigerator, etc.). You can decide what your standard is.

Another one is exercise. I don't advocate eliminating exercise entirely, because it's one of the best ways to increase your energy capacity. But let's face it, most of us are never going to run a marathon. I live on the route of the Chicago Marathon and every year I go out and watch those magnificent runners going by. But I don't want to be one of them. A couple of times a week I go out for a slow three-mile jog. I've been running the same distance at the same speed for thirty years. I am a mediocre runner.

Many people are fine with being mediocre cooks. Of course, some people eliminate cooking entirely and eat food cooked by others. But many people are fine with a few basic, easy recipes that don't take much time and provide adequate nourishment. Since I went to Italy for the first time and discovered what truly wonderful food tastes like, I have become passionate about good cooking. But that doesn't mean *you* have to be!

Accepting mediocrity in some parts of your life also makes delegation much easier. Sometimes the people to whom you delegate actually have higher standards than you do. My bookkeeper is much more fanatical about details than I am—thank goodness! But sometimes others don't do the task to the same standard you would. Are you going to micro-manage them to try to raise the quality of their work or accept what they are doing? The key question always is, "It is good enough?"

This is especially important when the person to whom you are delegating is a family member. If I ask my husband or my kids to do a task and then I criticize, micro-manage, or redo the task, that will really de-motivate them. Sometimes it's necessary to take a stand, but often—it's good enough. Let it go.

It's equally important in the workplace. As I discussed in chapter 3, one of the crucial aspects of being a manager is the ability to delegate. This is often especially hard for first-time managers (see https://www.ccl.org/articles/leading-effectively-articles/first-time-managers-must-conquer-these-challenges/). In most companies, you get promoted because you are good at *doing the job*. But as a manager, your task is to be good at *getting others to do the job*. Many, many first-time managers don't get this, and they drive their team nuts by continuing to intrude themselves into every detail of the work. What a waste of time and energy!

A manager is responsible for the quality of her team's work. But that doesn't mean she has to be involved in redoing every detail. She needs to be able to differentiate between the tasks that are mission-critical and all the rest of the work—where good enough is good enough.

For most people, mediocrity at work is harder to accept than mediocrity in our personal choices. This is equally true for men and women, sometimes for different reasons. For many men, their identity—their sense of self—is bound up in their work performance. They may be highly competitive, always keeping score and jostling with their peers for title, compensation, and scope of responsibility. For men like that, acknowledging that any part of their work product is just "good enough" can feel like failure.

There are certainly women who fit that same mold. But for many women, their striving for perfection stems from a different source. Especially if they work in male-dominated environments, women know that their work is often scrutinized more carefully and judged more harshly.[2] In those circumstances, women may feel that even the slightest compromise on the quality of their work will have devastating repercussions for them. And they may be right.

Once again, it's great to have high standards for your work. But perfection in everything is just not realistic. And when we attempt it, we are directing some of our precious energy toward relatively unimportant tasks at the expense of the really important ones. That is not a recipe for success, and it is not how the greatest leaders manage their time and energy.[3]

In your work world, there is the stuff that really matters—the tasks that define your role and determine whether or not you succeed. Figure out what those are and put your energy there. For the multitude of other tasks—good enough is good enough.

Rachel was a senior executive at a large communications agency. She had global responsibilities in a fast-paced, challenging field. When I first met Rachel, if you emailed her about *anything* you could be sure to get a response within five minutes. Sometimes I would message her and get the automatic response, "I am out of the office without access to email. I will respond as soon as possible when I return." And then within two minutes I would get Rachel's personal response.

It was great! I knew I would never have to wait around or send her a second message in order to get her answer. But Rachel's indiscriminate rule that she must *always* respond to any message within five minutes was making her a *less effective leader*. She would sit in meetings and respond to her email rather than paying attention to the people in the room. And she was teaching her colleagues and team members that they could always expect her to be at their beck and call, even about trivial matters.

After Rachel and I had worked for a while on curating her life, I noticed that I sometimes had to wait for a response from her. Sometimes I even had to ping her a second time. And you know, that was good enough!

Actually, email management has been a challenge for many of my clients. When I started working with Ashley, she had just been appointed director of Client Services in a large sales organization. She had already served in a number of managerial roles in the company, but she was new to the service organization and her team members were pretty skeptical about whether she was the right person for the job. Between that and the fact that superb client service had been identified as a key element in the company's strategy, Ashley was under a lot of pressure to show what she could do.

One of the first things Ashley told me was that she had three thousand emails in her in-box. That was because she was copied on just about every email that anyone sent to anyone within the Client Services department. Although she tried to keep up with the deluge, she had the good sense to recognize that her greatness did not lie in responding to the approximately sixty emails an hour

that poured in. So Ashley made several changes. She educated her
team about which emails she needed to see. She trained her assistant to perform triage on the emails so that about two-thirds of
them didn't even reach Ashley's eyes. But the reality was that even
so, keeping up with her emails was not going to make Ashley a
great leader. So she was secretly mediocre. She scanned some
emails, read very few, and deleted most of them without even
reading them. She taught her team to put "Mission Critical" into
the header if something really needed her attention. But even
then, there were too many for her to give her full attention to.

Funny thing—Ashley managed to do a great job as the director
of Client Services. Under her leadership, response time to client
requests shortened dramatically and complaints dropped. Satisfaction scores on the annual client survey increased significantly. And
all the time, *Ashley wasn't reading most of her emails*. Choosing to
be mediocre at responding to emails enabled her to be great at the
tasks that really mattered.

The mediocrity challenge is one part of curating your life
where that old bugaboo, "work-life balance," comes into play. It's
a hard fact that if you want to have a family and a fulfilling job,
you're going to have to cut corners in both spheres. Chances are
you are not going to win a Nobel Prize if you're busy looking after
young children. And you're probably not going to be the parent
who brings homemade cookies to school if you're a high-powered
neurosurgeon.

My client Sarah was trying to sort out this problem. She had
recently been promoted into her role as director of innovation for
a mid-size food services company. She had previously worked at a
huge, global consumer-packaged-goods company and was looking
forward to the opportunity for expanded scope and autonomy as a
leader in a smaller firm. From the beginning, her job required
long hours and frequent travel. Her work commitment was made
heavier by the fact that she lived about a three-hour drive from the
corporate headquarters. And to top it off, she had two young children at home.

Sarah's husband was great. He was a self-employed writer who set his own hours and he was willing to carry more than half of the responsibilities at home. But as the months went by, Sarah became more and more frustrated by how little time she was spending with her family. She spoke to her manager, who gave her permission to work from home on Fridays, which helped a lot.

And yet—less time at the office meant less time to build strategic relationships and participate in the informal networking and idea-sharing that was so necessary for her work. Sarah began to wonder whether she was doing her job even at a "good-enough" level, let alone the greatness she aspired to.

Sarah's story has a happy ending. She became one of the first women promoted to the C-suite (the most senior leadership team) in her company, even though she continued to spend at least one day a week at home. Although she still criticized her own performance, both at work and at home, the promotion provided her with the validation she needed to stay the course.

You will hear me say over and over again that curation is a very individual process. There is no one right way, and even the right ways have to change over time. But I'm going to step out of character for a moment and make a strong case for one particular curation decision.

If you have kids, there are no do-overs. You cannot disappear from your kid's life for extended periods of time and then just pick up the task later on. In my years as a clinician, I saw this over and over again. Depressed, lonely men in their mid-forties would come to see me. Although they had families, they had spent their children's early years focused almost entirely on building their own careers. They had often built fortunes, but their lives were emotionally impoverished. And here's the really tragic part—they were determined now to build more intimate relationships with their children. Meanwhile, their kids were now in their mid-teens, and they were not the slightest bit interested in getting closer to dear ol' Dad. I can tell you; those were some sad men.

When in doubt about where to put your best energy, choose your family. As the old cliché says, nobody ever says on his or her deathbed, "I wish I had spent more time at the office."

So what happens if you do choose to put your family first? Many of us really worry that if we slack off, it will affect how others see us. And sometimes it does. Does that matter? It depends. Figure 4.1 illustrates my framework for deciding where it's OK to choose mediocrity.

Cell 1 is easy—I'm going to do my very best on tasks that are highly important to me and to others who matter to me. Similarly, if I judge that a task really matters, I'm going to focus on it even if others' opinions are pretty irrelevant to me (cell 2). In some cases,

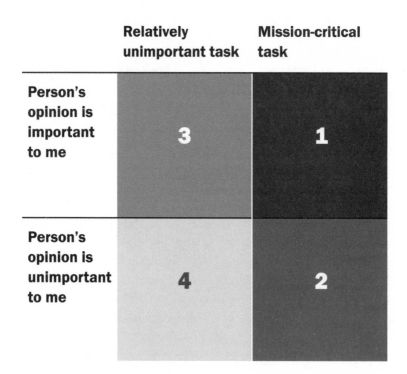

Figure 4.1. Choosing mediocrity. *Mary Clare Butler*

I'll put energy into a task that doesn't seem that big a deal to me because it really matters to someone I care about (cell 3).

But cell 4—that's the mediocrity sweet spot. If you're putting a lot of energy into tasks that really don't matter that much to you, and your critics are people you don't care much about, then it's time to ratchet your energy down. Of course, if you can say "no" to these tasks, that might be even better, but sometimes they really are mandatory.

Mary's house is pretty tidy now because she is an empty-nester. But when she had three young children running around (as well as half a dozen of their friends), her house was pretty much of a disaster. She felt constantly embarrassed about it and would often scurry around tidying up just before a guest came over. She never enjoyed housework, but she felt that she and her family should meet a high standard for housekeeping along with everything else they were doing.

And then one day she had a realization. She imagined that two people were talking about her and she could overhear their conversation without their knowledge. And she imagined that she heard, "You know that Mary? She's really good at her job and she helps a lot of people. Her kids are pretty great and her partner seems to love her. She's active in the community and generous to others. But, oh my goodness, have you seen their house?"

She realized she would be just fine with that. Her imagined critics were giving her high marks for the things that mattered to her and acknowledging that she was mediocre at something that was just not that important to her. After that, she stopped worrying so much about the toys all over her living room and the dishes in the sink and continued to use her energy for the things she really cared about.

What about if you are mediocre at something that really matters to you? First of all, figure out what it is that you care about—the product or the process? Then the short answer is:

- product—hire someone
- process—work at getting better at it.

Here's an example. I can prepare my own PowerPoint slides, but I'm not great at it and it takes me forever. It really matters to me that my slides look polished and professional—it's part of my brand. But I don't care if I myself am a great slide creator. So I pay a graphic artist to make my slides gorgeous and she does a terrific job. What's important to me is the product.

On the other hand, I want to be a great writer. So I work hard at it. I make it a priority. I set aside designated times for writing. I read other people's work to learn more about the craft of writing. I read and reread my own writing to make it better. I'm not going to hire a ghost writer to write my book for me. What matters to me is the process.

What happens if you refuse to be mediocre at anything? If instead, you insist that everything you do must be exceptional? I once assessed an executive who fell into that category. Seth was a talented, ambitious leader in a large retail company. He was a smart, quick-thinking problem solver who liked to tackle difficult challenges. But his perfectionism was becoming an increasing problem for him. His insistence on completing projects only to the highest standards worked very well in circumstances where attention to detail was critical. But he simply couldn't function in situations where "quick and dirty" was required. He worked very long hours and was having increasing difficulty managing the conflicting priorities in his work and home life. Seth was at risk of burning himself out, as well as driving his team and his colleagues crazy.

The bad news was that I could not recommend Seth for a promotion he desired. I knew that his perfectionism would become even more problematic as his scope of responsibilities broadened. He was very disappointed and hurt when he wasn't selected. The good news was that he reacted by hiring a coach who helped him to see how he was getting in his own way. Over the next year he made progress toward setting priorities and accepting lower standards in some areas of his work. You might think that becoming "mediocre" would arrest Seth's career progress, but in fact the opposite happened. He focused his energy on his key objectives and—Abracadabra!—his productivity increased and he earned his sought-after promotion.

Choosing mediocrity is one of the key differentiators between curating your life and other approaches to "work-life balance." It sounds so awful—as if you're a slob who doesn't care about the quality of your work. Giving yourself permission to be mediocre is probably the hardest part of curation for most people. It's important to remember our model of the museum curator who has to select what goes into her exhibit. Some objects don't make it into the exhibit at all. A few are featured very prominently. And most of the items are in the side rooms where people can look at them if they want to. Those side rooms are our "Halls of Mediocrity," the places where we do just enough and no more.

The truth is—most of what we do in life is mediocre! It's OK, it's good enough. Making those choices consciously and deliberately enables us to use most of our energy for the things that really matter, the things we want to be great at. Let's talk about that next.

KEY TAKEAWAYS

- Expecting yourself to be perfect at everything is a recipe for failure.
- The good is not the enemy of the great. The good is the friend of the great. By settling for good, or even mediocre, in some parts of your life, you free up your energy to become great at the really important activities.
- Consciously and deliberately choose where you will be mediocre.
- You don't have to tell people what you have chosen to be mediocre at. Most of the time they won't notice.
- Don't worry about the carrots.

5

CHOOSE GREATNESS

I was in tenth grade when I had Miss Goluch for Accelerated English class. She was an outstanding teacher—interesting, challenging, and full of energy. I, on the other hand, was a well-behaved but cocky student. I was used to getting top grades without doing a lot of work. One day Miss Goluch handed back one of my papers with the usual high mark. But this time she looked at me and said, "Gail, this paper is good enough to get an A in my class. But you could do a lot better."

I was taken aback. I was used to teachers telling me how wonderful my work was. Miss Goluch's words stung. But at the same time, they were a challenge to me. Why wasn't I producing the work that was the best I could do?

This encounter changed my life. Miss Goluch challenged me to bring my best to my work, whether others required it of me or not. As you know if you have read the previous chapters, that doesn't mean I always do my best on every project I undertake. Sometimes good enough is good enough. But after Miss Goluch's class, taking pride in my work—in making it *great*—became a much bigger part of my value system.

It makes me sad to think about a life with no greatness in it. I know there are many people who can't think about greatness— they're thinking about survival. You may have heard about Abraham Maslow and his model of the hierarchy of needs.[1] Maslow was a psychologist in the twentieth century who came up with the concept of self-actualization, which he defined as the fulfillment of the need for meaning in your life. Maslow recognized that people couldn't become self-actualized unless more fundamental needs had been met, as illustrated in Figure 5.1.

Maslow's message was that if you're starving or in danger or no one loves you or respects you, you're not going to be able to work on finding meaning in your life until you have figured out how to satisfy those more basic needs.

Like many theories that have been around for a while, Maslow's theory has its detractors. But I continue to find it a useful way to think about human needs and priorities. It also helps me to remember that many of the problems I deal with are "first-world problems." They are very real and significant for people like me

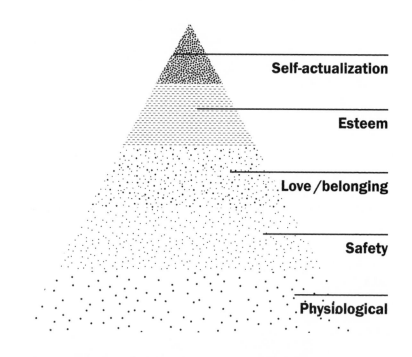

Figure 5.1.   Maslow's hierarchy of needs. *Mary Clare Butler*

who don't have to worry about survival, but that's not everyone. I am never going to criticize someone who isn't worried about meaning in her work because she's focused on feeding her children.

But for those of us who are fortunate enough to be well-fed, safe, loved, and respected, the search for meaning is important. And when I talk about greatness, it's connected to meaning. *This whole book is about being great at the things that matter to you— the things that have meaning.*

Here's an example of finding the meaning in your work. Emma was the managing director of the most profitable office of a global consulting firm. She oversaw the work of hundreds of people and was responsible for a budget larger than that of most mid-size companies. The revenue from her office supported the work at a number of lower-performing offices. Emma was a phenomenally hard worker who constantly kept her eye on the prize. But in her rapidly changing industry, it was also essential for her to sometimes step back from the daily operations to focus on bigger-picture questions. Where is our industry going? What sorts of skill sets do we need to look for in our new hires? Are we staying ahead of our clients? Where are we leaving money on the table? Who are our most threatening competitors?

It was really hard for Emma to find the time to focus on these questions because she had so many other responsibilities. So we agreed that she would carve out half a day for the two of us to meet and explore some of these questions together. As we were digging through some of these problems, it seemed to me that Emma wasn't fully engaged in what we were doing. So I asked her, "Emma, what would happen if the industry you are in didn't exist? What difference would it make?"

Emma was startled by the question, and she was silent for several minutes. Then she laid out a very clear picture of what would be lost if nobody did the work her company was doing. She was able to articulate why her work *mattered.* Our conversation continued with renewed energy and by the end of our session Emma had come up with some critical insights to take back to her work. She told me later that my question and her answer provided her with a new sense of the value of her work and empowered her to take some bold steps forward.

Being great is about doing work that matters.

Greatness is not fame. You *may* be famous for what you are great at. But there are lots of people who are famous for something other than greatness. Mrs. O'Leary is famous for starting the Great Chicago Fire. (She probably didn't, but that's another story.) Steve Bartman is famous for catching a foul ball that caused the Chicago Cubs to lose a game and possibly the National League pennant that year. Monica Lewinsky is famous for being the victim of sexual harassment. All of these people may be great at something, but that's not what they're famous for.

And you can be truly great in ways that no one knows about. My favorite examples of this come from my years as a therapist. I frequently had clients who had survived absolutely awful childhood experiences—abuse, neglect, parental alcoholism, and the like. They had every reason to be completely emotionally disabled. And yet—they had formed loving relationships, they held down jobs, they were productive members of the community. Sure, they were struggling with their emotional scars—but they were making good lives for themselves and the people around them.

How were they doing it? Where did they find the strength and resilience to rise above their horrible early experiences? I asked them those very questions. And every single time, the client would say, "There was this person who made a difference to me. She (or he) made me welcome in her home. She made me feel I was worth something. She believed in me." The person was often a neighbor or a teacher.

Those are the people who change the trajectory of a child's life. They *saved* that child. And not only will they never be famous for what they did—they probably don't even realize how significant it was. In my mind, that is true greatness. And it only happened because those people were willing to use their energy to be good to some ragamuffin who kept showing up at their door or sat in the back of their classroom.

Of course, sometimes people do indeed become famous for their greatness—athletes, artists, business and political leaders, heroes, and others. But greatness and fame are not the same thing.

When I was a girl, I was terrified of being ordinary. To me that seemed like the worst fate in the world. I wanted to be the first Jewish woman president of the United States. I wanted to win the Nobel Peace Prize. I wanted to be a famous actress. I am now at the stage of my life when I have to recognize that I will be none of those things.

The good news is that I am no longer terrified of being ordinary, because I know that ordinary people can do great things. I was stunned a couple of years ago when my son, Ben, wrote a piece on Facebook about *Star Wars*. As you probably know, part of the *Star Wars* saga is that an infant, Luke Skywalker, is fostered by a farming couple, Owen and Beru, on a backwater planet, Tatooine. Luke grows up and leaves Tatooine to become a famous galactic warrior, while Owen and Beru die horrible deaths and are neither remembered nor celebrated. Here is what Ben wrote:

> At some point in history, someone needed to convince young men to leave their families and go to war, which must've been a super tough sell. They wrote stories glorifying battle. To sell war. The stories never went away. They got tweaked and now also sell entrepreneurship. The force (pun intended) of these stories is really hard to counteract. You have to argue Owen and Beru's life is better than Luke's. The real life Owens and Berus are people who've, say, been married 30+ years, lived in the same house for 20+. *They're winning* (emphasis mine). Being a billionaire/famous/having political power maybe is actually stressful and not that fun. Maybe we stop celebrating that life?

There were two things that surprised me about Ben's perspective. First, I would have predicted that, as a young man, Ben would have found Luke's adventures much more impressive than Owen and Beru's mundane life and quiet courage. Second, I was deeply touched that he was validating his father's and my life choices.

The point is not that we should all be rural foster parents, or that no one should seek money or fame or power. The point is there are many different kinds of greatness. And if you are fortunate enough to be at the self-actualization level of Maslow's pyramid, you need to figure out what *your* greatness will be—and put your energy there.

A major reorganization in his company was the stimulus for Arjun to think about his greatness. He was in a mid-level management role in a huge global health care organization when the whole leadership landscape changed around him. Anyone who has worked for a big corporation knows that major re-orgs are fairly frequent occurrences, and they are usually hugely disruptive to the lives of the employees. For one thing, re-orgs usually involve firings and lay-offs as roles and structures are redesigned. So re-orgs are scary and often provoke defensiveness and resistance on the part of employees as they struggle to maintain their power and their routines.

Arjun was different. He saw the re-org as an opportunity to reevaluate what kind of leader he wanted to be. He had been focusing his energy on two main goals: being an excellent people leader and getting the job done. He was known for the positive climate on his team and for his outstanding skills in execution.

But Arjun's passion was innovation. He wanted to move beyond following through on others' creative initiatives and make himself and his team into an innovative force. So, in the upheaval of the re-org, he negotiated a new role for himself where he would have the opportunity to participate in and contribute to some of the company's most innovative work. It was an intimidating move for him and really stretched him out of his comfort zone. He focused on learning from the innovative people around him, freeing up his thought processes, and taking bigger risks in his work. And it paid off. Arjun went on to lead one of the company's most impactful initiatives. Part of what made this so gratifying for him was that while he was focusing more of his energy on being great at innovation, his long-term skills in people management and execution also contributed to his outstanding success. Arjun is a shining example of how someone can use a change in his external circumstances to advance his own journey to greatness.

Choosing greatness doesn't require you to focus on only one thing. For many of us, greatness at one thing is enough. But for others, that kind of single-mindedness doesn't feel right. Sofia is a good example. Sofia was a very talented flutist. She practiced hard throughout her childhood, won awards in music competitions, and was accepted into a prestigious conservatory. After she graduated, she made a good career as a freelance musician, playing in orchestras, chamber ensembles, and other gigs. She also began teaching private students.

In the lessons, Sofia gradually realized that she wasn't working only on her students' musical technique. At times they would come to the lessons with other troubles on their minds which affected their concentration and how they played. At other times as she was working with a student on how to interpret a particular piece of music, aspects of the students' personalities, hopes, or fears would emerge and become part of the process.

Over the next several years, Sofia became increasingly interested in how psychological factors affected her students' musical development. Eventually she went back to school, earned a master's degree in psychology, and became a psychotherapist—a good one. She built a private practice and became a powerful and effective healer.

And she never stopped playing the flute. She continued to work on her own musical skills, performed regularly, and wrote some beautiful compositions. Sofia became great in two very different spheres, and each one contributed to the other.

Some people have a different problem—they are gifted and talented at so many different things that they have difficulty focusing on one or two. You may not be initially very sympathetic to these folks. "Really, that's a problem—being too good at too many things? I wish I had that problem." But surprisingly, it can actually be quite stressful. Some people believe if they have a gift, they are obligated to use it. So what do you do if you are a skilled hockey player, a whiz at video games, a talented guitar player, fluent in four languages, and an outstanding cook? How do you give yourself permission to pull back from some of your gifts and focus on one or two? Of course, you can still keep doing all those activities, but you'll almost certainly have to settle for just "good" in most of them so you can focus your energy on the one or two where your greatness lies.

You don't have to choose just one thing to be great at, although many people do. You're pretty unlikely to be great at ten things. But many people have more than one greatness goal. However, another challenge is that sometimes those goals are incompatible. My client Ed was dealing with that problem. Ed had identified two greatness goals that were really important to him.

First, although he was a very intelligent man who had excelled in a variety of business leadership roles, he had never earned a college degree—and it bugged him. It's funny—I find that people who have advanced degrees often minimize their importance. They even sometimes seem apologetic about all their schooling. But for some people, not having a college degree makes them feel inferior. Ed was one of those people—it mattered to him to have those letters after his name. It also mattered to his manager, who had told him that he would not be able to advance to a higher level in the company without a degree. Ed had been exploring different academic programs and was hoping to start taking courses soon.

But Ed also had a second goal. He had been severely overweight all his life, and he was determined to lose weight and become strong and fit. His doctor had warned him that his health would be compromised if he didn't lose some weight and get stronger. He knew that for him, weight loss would require a high level of discipline and a serious commitment to spending time in the gym.

Of course, Ed wanted to do both—earn his BA and get physically fit. But he had the good sense to recognize that it was unrealistic to attempt both at the same time, given that he had a demanding full-time job and family responsibilities. He didn't want to accept that constraint, but eventually he decided that his health had to take priority. For a seriously overweight person to change his body type and maintain that change—that takes greatness! And somewhere down the road, when he had tackled that challenge, then he could reconsider going to college.

How do you figure out what your greatness will be? Sometimes people think about this in terms of *legacy*. What do I want to be remembered for? What have I accomplished, or what will I accomplish, that I am truly proud of? Carl Reiner, the ninety-seven-year-old comedian, writer, actor, and director, appeared in a documentary, *If You're Not in the Obit, Eat Breakfast*. I'm not as old as Reiner, and I hope to live many more years, but I also have the habit of reading the obituaries. I am fascinated by what people are remembered for. Here are a few edited quotes from a recent local paper:

- She was the first professional librarian in the school system. As computers were coming in, she learned everything about computers and helped the kids learn it all.
- She passed away artfully hand-making her final set of Christmas cards for her legion of lifelong friends near and far.
- He was a former Alderman, a member of Kiwanis Club, and a retired attorney.
- She wrote, "The world is a beautiful place and people are people no matter where they are from."
- He spent his entire career in public accounting and loved his clients and coworkers.

It fascinates me—the variety of those choices of greatness. Of course, most obituaries are entirely about the deceased's relationships with family and close friends. For many, many people, our family relationships and close friendships are the most important part of our lives. Is that where your greatness resides? Then you'd better make sure that you are investing your best energy in those relationships and not letting them be pushed aside for other activities that are not as important to you.

For myself, I have thought about what I have accomplished in my life so far that I am most proud of. Here's my list. I enabled my husband to do the work he loves and was born to do. I raised three amazing sons. I helped a lot of people through my work as a psychologist. I was a leader in expanding opportunities for women to participate fully in the religious observances at my synagogue. And I had the courage to make a major career change in the middle of my career.

I'm not dead yet, and I don't plan on dying anytime soon. I want to add some more achievements I can feel really proud of—who knows, maybe this book. Looking back over what you have done that feels meaningful and important is one way of getting clear about what you want to do next.

Believe it or not, it's break time again. Time sure flies when you're reading a terrific book. How about doing some stretches? Stand up on your tip-toes, roll your neck, pull your shoulders back. If you get really ambitious, you could try to touch your toes or stand on one foot.

A second consideration to help you choose your greatness is *capability.* I want to inject a realistic note here. I do not subscribe to the belief that anyone can do anything if they just *want* it enough. I know many people who wanted to be truly great at something, who worked really hard at it, and who were never able to master it. Sometimes they felt good that they had made the effort and sometimes they felt really stupid.

Ed was a highly intelligent young man who wanted to be a physicist. He went to an elite university where the physics department was notoriously demanding. He failed his first physics course, but he kept trying. He failed it again, and he failed the next one he tried. Ed kept taking physics courses for three years, and he failed every single one. So he dropped out of university and traveled for several years, working at odd jobs along the way. During that break he realized that although he longed to be a great physicist, that was not where his intelligence lay. His gift was lan-

guages. He returned to university and majored in French literature. He was a brilliant success and went on to an impressive
career as a writer and editor in several languages. He felt foolish
that he had wasted several years of his youth pursuing an utterly
unrealistic goal. But that did not stop him from reevaluating and
finding the path to his true greatness.

My observation is that when people have regrets, they are usually much more about the possibilities they did *not* pursue than
about the efforts that failed. As the great hockey star Wayne
Gretzky famously put it, "You miss 100% of the shots you never
take." https://www.forbes.com/sites/actiontrumpseverything/2014/
01/12/you-miss-100-of-the-shots-you-dont-take-so-start-shooting-
at-your-goal/#5396c4c06a40.

A recent psychological study explored what people most often
regret.[2] The Big Five regrets were: choosing the wrong life partner; dropping out of college; trying too hard to please others instead of following their own path; living too cautiously; and not
saving enough money. While each person chooses his or her
unique path, it's interesting that we tend to make many of the
same mistakes. Pay attention to avoiding the Big Five, because
regret is one of the most painful feelings—that sense of having
made the wrong choice with no chance now to fix it. *Think about
what makes you feel regret and then live your life making the
choices that minimize the likelihood that you will feel it again.*

If you're not sure where your greatness lies, sometimes that
means you have to engage in *experimentation.* You have to try out
a few different paths to discover where your capabilities and passion intersect. A few people find greatness in childhood or adoles-
cence, but for many people, early adulthood is the time when they
are most free to engage in this kind of experimentation. They have
relatively few obligations and a long runway ahead of them to
course-correct if the path isn't working for them.

I am a strong advocate of young people having the freedom to
explore different paths, especially when they are still in school. I
was lucky to do my undergraduate work at the University of Chicago, a school that has long been an advocate for broad undergrad-

uate education. I took courses in geography, Indian civilization, cellular biology, calculus, and many other fascinating subjects along with classes in my major, psychology. Although I didn't pursue those other paths, I was grateful to have the opportunity to explore them before narrowing my education when I went to graduate school.

Experimentation doesn't end when you leave school. Devin is a good example. He became interested in community theater as a teenager and decided he wanted to become a professional actor. He worked hard to master his craft in a prestigious undergraduate theater program and then spent a year as a working actor in regional theater productions. He loved the work but realized the pay was so low that he couldn't support himself, let alone the family he wanted to have someday. So, like many other young people with a dream of acting stardom, he headed out to Hollywood.

It didn't take him long to reach a shocking realization—he didn't want to be an actor after all! He became fascinated with screenwriting. As Devin put it, "I don't just want to be part of someone else's puzzle, I want to create my own." What now? He began to write—stories, short scripts, all sorts of stuff. He took a couple of courses. He hung out with writers and producers and directors of independent films. And he waited tables.

Ten years later, Devin was still in Hollywood. He had built a great network of friends and colleagues. He had written and produced several films that had earned some critical respect. He had learned how to do sound production and was making money at that, so he only had to wait tables a couple of nights a week. He still hadn't had his big break. But he was having fun, doing good work, and making enough money to live on. The experiment continued.

There must be something about the arts that makes this kind of story common, because Martin is another good example. He grew up in a family of very talented visual artists—painters and sculptors. His parents were seriously committed to their artistic projects, but they earned their money at other jobs. Martin followed in their footsteps, getting early training in art and working hard to get good at it. His talent was apparent early and his work got some notice. But he did not plan on making a living as an artist.

When Martin went to college, he majored in chemistry. He was a good student and he found chemistry very interesting. But people who knew him well were puzzled, because it was clear that while he liked chemistry just fine, he *loved* making art. After college, Martin decided to take a year off school before deciding on his next step. It was during that year that he realized he really had to pursue art seriously. His parents were horrified—no one in the family was a professional artist, and they knew full well how difficult it was to succeed. But Martin was afraid that if he didn't take a serious shot at being an artist, he would wake up at the age of forty-five and feel he had missed the boat. So Martin went to art school, earned a master's degree in fine arts, and set out to build a career as an artist.

It was a tough road, but he persisted. He combined his artistic work with teaching jobs, and over time he was recognized as a gifted artist and was able to make a living. Martin is now at retirement age and he jokes that he is still trying out art as a career. If it doesn't work out, he can always go back to chemistry.

I don't want to leave the topic of choosing greatness without spending a little time on tools that can help you figure out what you're good at. There is a multitude of tools that have been developed to help people evaluate their talents and abilities. Keep in mind that most of them are designed specifically for making decisions about your career, as opposed to greatness defined more broadly.

This kind of assessment is not my area of specialty, so I asked some of my colleagues what tests they use. Please note that I have not done a thorough study of the research underlying these tools, but they are in common use among experienced professional career counselors. Here are some examples of assessments that can help to identify where your abilities lie:

- *Profiles PXT*: This tool is a pre-employment screening tool designed to help employers select the job candidates who are the best fit for specific jobs, based on their core behaviors. It can also be used by individuals who want to know more about the kinds of jobs they are best suited for. For more information, check out https://www.profilesinternational.com/.

- *Pathfinders*: This tool helps people learn about their natural talents, which will help them to target their best career paths. For more information, see http://pathfinderscareerdesign.com/professional-career-aptitude-test-to-find-your-strengths/.

- *The Strong Interest Inventory*: This tool is one of the older and more established career coaching tools. It helps people find their best-fit career. The assessment has been revised to stay current by examining people's interests and matching them with up-to-date careers. Learn more at https://careerassessmentsite.com/tests/career-tests/strong-interest-inventory-career-tests/.

- *CliftonStrengths Assessment*: The assessment measures people's natural patterns of thinking, feeling, and behaving, so when they have completed the test, they will have discovered their talents. For more information, check out https://www.gallupstrengthscenter.com/home/en-us/cliftonstrengths-how-it-works.

- *MRG Personal Directions*: This assessment measures "life architecture" and "quality of life" variables to provide people with feedback on how they see themselves in significant areas of their lives. This provides a foundation for both career development and personal growth to foster individual success at work and in life. *Personal Directions* provides information on what people want from their world, where they have invested their energy, how they feel about those investments, and actions to consider for future choices. See more at https://www.mrg.com/assessments/personal-growth/.

- *MBTI 2*: This tool is a revision of an assessment that has been around for a long time. It classifies people into sixteen types which provide information about how people prefer to get their energy, take in information, make decisions, and organize their lives. That enables them to approach their work in a way best suited to their style, including how to manage their time, problem solve, make decisions, and deal with stress. For more information, see https://www. myersbriggs.org/type-use-for-everyday-life/mbti-type-at-work/.

- *Kolbe*: This index classifies people into four types: Fact Finder, Follow Through, Quick Start, and Implementer, which provides guidance on the kinds of tasks and environments which will be the best fit for them. See http://www. kolbe.com/.
- *Predictive Index*: This assessment measures four traits: dominance, extraversion, patience, and formality. These are then used to provide guidance about job fit. More information is at https://www.predictiveindex.com/.
- *Highland's Ability Battery*: This assessment provides feedback on three dimensions: Personal Style, Driving Abilities, and Specialized Abilities, which can then provide career direction. Check out https://www.highlandsco.com/.

There are many more tools out there. The good ones usually cost something and often require that you speak with a consultant to interpret the results. These tests can provide very useful information to guide your search for where your greatness lies. But they will not replace spending time reflecting on what you know about yourself and getting information from the people around you who know you well.

So far, I've talked about two dimensions of how people choose greatness: legacy and capability. The third one is *passion*. You may be really good at something. You may even believe that doing that activity would create a meaningful legacy. But without passion, it will be very hard for you to put in the determined, sustained effort we'll be talking about in the next chapter. Without passion, it will be agonizing to make the required sacrifices—saying no to other wonderful choices in order to focus on your chosen path.

Keith Ferrazzi summarizes this very well in his book, *Never Eat Alone*.[3] He talks about the "blue flame"—the intersection between passion and ability. Find your blue flame—figure out where your greatness lies—and then go for it, full force.

KEY TAKEAWAYS

- Be great at the things that matter to you—the things that have meaning.
- Greatness is not the same as fame.
- Figure out what your greatness is and put your energy there.
- Do experiments.
- It is not true that you can be great at anything if you just want it enough.
- Think about what makes you feel regret and then live your life making the choices that minimize the likelihood that you will feel it again.
- Choosing greatness is based on legacy, capability, and passion.

6

LIVE YOUR GREATNESS

Living your greatness requires three ingredients: *talent, opportunity, and fierce dedication.* We talked about talent in the last chapter. You don't have much control over talent. That's a gift. Your only job is to figure out where your talent lies.

You also have limited control over your opportunities. You were born when and where you were born, into the family you were born into, and that reality has a huge influence on whether you'll be great at one thing or another. Malcolm Gladwell's book *Outliers* talks about how much your circumstances influence whether you'll be great and what you'll be great at.[1] For example, it is entirely possible that one of my sons could have been an extraordinary athlete. He is strong and muscular, coordinated, and energetic. He enjoys athletic activity and is good at almost every sport he tries. But since my husband and I don't have a great interest in sports, we didn't encourage our sons to participate in them with any kind of focus or intensity. No great athletes have sprung from the Golden family tree.

Some people may argue that you can create your own opportunities, and to a certain extent I agree. But let's face it—if you are born in a favela in Rio di Janeiro, you'll have different opportunities than if you are born in a mansion in Winnetka, Illinois. There are remarkable people who rise above their circumstances, but for most of us, those circumstances either lift us up or pose pretty ferocious barriers.

A few years ago, I attended a fascinating workshop on diversity led by Verna Myers. She led us through an exercise about "privilege." We all stood in a straight line beside each other as she named various life circumstances, such as:

- I grew up in a middle-class home.
- My parents were college educated.
- I have had no significant medical challenges.
- I have never been the victim of serious violence.

Each time the sentence was true for you, you took a step forward. After about ten of these items, we looked around and realized that some of us were much farther ahead than others. All the people in that room were successful professionals, so the exercise demonstrated two things—that we come from very different levels of opportunity and that, as a result, some of us are going to have an easier time getting to our greatness.

It's important to remember that. Otherwise, you'll be someone who was "born on third base and thinks he hit a triple."

As I said, in general, you don't have much control over your talents or your opportunities. But—*you do have control over what you will dedicate yourself to*. My husband trains musicians, and he assures me that the students' work ethic and passion are much more predictive of their musical trajectory than their raw talent is. When my son, Aaron, entered drama school, his professors told him and his classmates, "You are all very talented or you wouldn't be here. So are thousands of other people. What will make the difference is how hard you work at your craft."

A client of mine, Jada, is a good example of seizing an opportunity and dedicating herself to it. She was a very senior executive in line to become the next CEO of the global firm where she worked. To her disappointment, the Board of Directors chose one of her competitors for the CEO role. However, the company valued Jada's abilities very highly and wanted to keep her, so the new

CEO and the Board created a new role for her. The problem was that the role was very vague and undefined. Jada was dismayed—she felt as if she had been put out to pasture. But within a couple of months she had identified a key strategic initiative that was critically important to the company's success. She assembled a team, explored the opportunity, and convinced the Executive Leadership Team to support the initiative. She and her team created some highly innovative intellectual property for the company that proved to be of great value. Jada's success came because she figured out what she was great at and matched that to what the company needed. Instead of allowing herself to be defeated by losing the promotion and finding herself in an undefined role, she utilized her intellect and energy to do something great.

So figure out what you want to be great at. Consider your talents and your circumstances. And then *dedicate* yourself to those endeavors. Here are some things you will need to consider in your quest for greatness.

- *What kind of effort will this work require?* Is it a daily commitment? Does it take bursts of effort? Will the work be predictable or not? The answers to these questions will provide guidance on how to manage your energy to tackle the challenge.
- *What do I have to learn to be great at this?* Do I need to go to school? Find a teacher? Teach myself? Unlearn what I've already learned?
- *How will I stay great?* Is this a one-time achievement like climbing Mount Everest, or do I want to sustain my greatness for decades? How will I keep in shape, stay open, not get stale?
- *What tools do I need to become/stay great?* How can I get access to the things I need?
- *What support do I need from other people?* There certainly are individuals who do extraordinary things without much obvious support from others. But it is almost always the case that you will not become great alone. You will need teachers,

cheerleaders, critics, financial backers, friends and lovers, an audience, trusted advisors and so on.

When I started my company in May 2009, the American economy was in terrible shape. I had been downsized by the consulting firm I was working for, and it took me only a week to figure out that if I wanted to work, I would have to create my own job. So I started Gail Golden Consulting and set out to build my company. I was terrified, hurt, and lonely. But a remarkable thing started to happen. People I barely knew began offering me help—free office space in downtown Chicago, invaluable advice about marketing, useful introductions, and contacts. Even my hairstylist, Carolyn Bakken, offered to cut my hair for half-price until I landed on my feet. When I was about to make a foolish career choice, one of my former colleagues, Mazy Gillis, advised me, "Gail, good decisions are rarely made out of fear." I followed her good guidance and stayed the course, working on building Gail Golden Consulting.

Within a few months I had some clients and was off and running. Now, more than ten years later, my company is successful, as measured by the three questions I learned from John Blattner—Am I having fun? Am I doing good work? Am I making money? I would not be where I am without the incredible generosity of those people who helped me in those dark early months—and who have kept on helping me.

They paid it forward. It's a cliché, I know, but it's the best way to describe what people did for me in those early months. Paying it forward has become a fundamental part of my business practice. Your kid needs some career counseling? Sure. You're starting a new small business and need some advice? Of course.

Don't get me wrong. Most of the time I get paid well for the work I do. I can't afford to give away all my services, and I suspect you can't either. But I didn't get where I am without enormous help from others—and I am therefore obligated to extend that same generosity to others.

The last point you need to consider in your quest for greatness is:

- *How do I measure greatness?* You need to know what greatness looks like for you. Is it running a hundred marathons? Making a million dollars? Being on the front page of *Fortune* magazine? Raising young adults who know how to love and to work? Experiencing the Divine? In order to dedicate yourself to your greatness, you need to have a vision of what it looks like when you get there.

Part of living your greatness is getting very clear about the right metric to focus on. My client, Jesse, is a good example. Jesse was a senior associate in a large law firm who was working very hard to become a partner. His goal was to become a powerful leader in the firm who provided great client service, contributed to the firm's success, and held authority and influence with his colleagues.

Jesse knew that a key part of becoming a partner was bringing in new business for the firm and expanding existing accounts. He had an appealing, energetic interpersonal style and enjoyed business networking. His colleagues admired his energy in getting involved in community organizations. But there was a problem. Jesse was putting huge amounts of his energy into making his network as large as possible. He measured his success by the *number* of new contacts he made at an event. But that metric was irrelevant to his goal. He needed to be focusing on the *quality* of those contacts—how likely they were to generate business for the firm. Once he figured out how he was missing the mark by measuring the wrong thing, he was able to rethink his networking strategy, bring in more business, and make partner within the next two years.

As you measure your own greatness, it's important to give yourself *time to become great.* Many of the clients I work with are extremely critical and demanding, both of themselves and of others. If you insist that you must always be great at your work, then it's very hard to try anything new. Almost no one is great when they're just starting to learn to do something.

My client Andre is a good example. Andre was one of the most impressive young executives I have ever worked with. He was handsome, very smart, and well-spoken. He had a quiet confidence that made him seem older than his years. He was a superb problem solver and a really good people leader.

I met Andre when he was identified as a high-potential leader at Green Company, a global manufacturing corporation. He was part of a cohort of young leaders who had been selected for a special program to fast-track their leadership development and groom them for specific promotions. Andre was promoted in short order and continued to perform very well. But he was ambitious and could not see a path within the company that would lead where he wanted to go.

So several years later, when I was no longer consulting to Green Company, I was delighted to learn that Andre was being considered for a senior leadership role at Yellow Company, where I was now a consultant. I was asked to provide a candidate assessment of Andre, and I was happy to recommend him for the role. When Andre was brought on board, I was asked to be his integration coach.

By then, Andre was even more capable and polished than when I had worked with him at Green Company and I knew he was positioned for success. But here was the challenge. Yellow Company was in an entirely different industry from Green Company. Although Andre's experience at Green Company had helped to prepare him for the new role, he had a *lot* to learn about the new industry. If he came in on Day One expecting to be great in his new role, he was going to disappoint himself and annoy his new colleagues. He had to put in the time and the work to become as great in this role as he had been in his previous one.

Good news—I was able to help Andre see the importance of taking his time to learn the new landscape. He managed his impatience and his self-critical style effectively and he quickly became a high-powered leader at Yellow Company. A few years later he was offered the C-suite role of his dreams at Chartreuse Company, where once again he was wise enough to allow himself the time to grow into his greatness.

It's really important to give yourself time to become great. And it's equally important to know when it's time to step back from it. We've all met people who peaked in high school. They were the captain of the football team and the Prom King and they've been living on that glory ever since. I've heard so many writers and professors talking about important work they did—decades ago. When you hang on to your past greatness you become a shadow of yourself, and sometimes an object of pity.

What's the alternative? Honor your past successes and achievements—and move on to new ones. Richard Rodgers, the great songwriter, wrote a lyric about how the sweetest sounds he would ever hear were still inside his head. He didn't just keep playing his wonderful old songs. He worked to get new "sweetest sounds" out of his head and onto paper so the rest of us could enjoy them, too.

Many years ago, I had the remarkable experience of hearing B. F. Skinner speak at a conference of the American Psychological Association. Skinner was one of the giants of behavioral psychology, a hugely influential thinker and researcher. He had amply demonstrated his greatness. But in his speech, he told us about a very distressing experience. He had written an article about a topic that interested him and then discovered to his dismay that he had already written the same article many years earlier. He realized that as he aged he was at risk of repeating himself. What did he do? He set off to research a completely different area of psychology, so there was no chance that he would fall into that repetitive trap. In my mind, that's greatness.

If you are going to live your greatness, there will be times when you fail, times when you take a risk and it doesn't pan out, times when you feel defeated. At times like that you will need to demonstrate resilience, the ability to bounce back from difficult experiences.

April showed entrepreneurial energy from a young age. As a child she watched her mother baking cookies and decided she would start a cookie business. It didn't last long, but she had fun with it and pleased a few customers. In high school, she hung around a scuba shop chatting up the customers until the manager made her a sales person. She was in college when she started her first real business providing IT consultation, and she poured her heart into the business. In fact, she dropped out after two years so she could work full-time on the business and she gave it everything she had. She ate ramen, lived in a basement, and worked like a fiend.

The business failed. April barely skipped a beat. Within a few months she had decided to go back to college—and start another business. She took the lessons she had learned from her first failure, did it better the second time around, and that business is still thriving. That's resilience.

The American Psychological Association says that resilience is not a trait that you have or don't have—it's a set of behaviors and thoughts that can be learned (see https://www.apa.org/helpcenter/road-resilience). I agree—with this reservation: if you have experienced a whole bunch of setbacks in short order, your resilience will probably be diminished. Some of the behaviors that are associated with resilience include taking decisive action, developing a positive view of yourself, and maintaining a hopeful outlook. Resilience is increased by making use of your strong social connections to help you through the tough times instead of suffering in silence and isolation.

Here it is, break time again. How about a little snack—maybe a piece of fruit or a handful of nuts? Be sure to get up and move around. Think about something pleasing—a place you've been that makes you happy or an event you're looking forward to.

Whatever greatness goal you have chosen, you have to get to work and make it happen. Sometimes that's joyful and fun, passionately pursuing an activity that really matters to you. Sometimes it's brutally hard, because to get where you want to go you have to do things that are not intrinsically fun or satisfying.

David was a self-employed artist. He loved his work. He had all three of the requirements for greatness—talent, opportunity, and dedication. But he worked alone much of the time, with little feedback or encouragement from others. There were days when he had great difficulty focusing on his art. He read the paper, wandered into the kitchen to get a snack, looked at some stuff online, found a home improvement project that needed his attention, sent an email to an old friend, had another snack, ordered some supplies he needed, looked at some more stuff online—you get the picture. We were talking about curation and he asked me, "What do you do about procrastination? How do you make yourself work even when you don't feel like it?" Or as one of my colleagues put it, how do you achieve "nocrastination?"

Fortunately, psychologists have done a lot of research on how to motivate people. Often the research focuses on how to motivate other people, but the same techniques can help to motivate yourself.

Here are a few of the techniques that have proven effective:

- rewards and punishments
- breaking down the task
- visualizing the goal
- making a public commitment
- developing routines or habits
- social self-regulation
- cultivating a learning-goal (mastery) orientation
- interrupting counterproductive habits

Let's discuss them in more detail.

Rewards and punishments. Psychology as a science has been around since the early 1900s, although it really took off after World War II. In the hundred-plus years that psychologists have been studying human behavior, one finding is by far the most consistent. *If you want someone to do more of something, reward them when they do it.* There are all kinds of complexities about what constitutes a reward for whom, how big the reward should be, what reward schedule works best, intrinsic vs. extrinsic rewards, and so on. But we know for a fact that reward is the most powerful tool for modifying human behavior—our own and others.

So one way to get yourself to do what you need to do is to create a reward for yourself. If I work on this difficult task for the next ninety minutes without fooling around, I get to have a cookie, or take a walk, or listen to a podcast, or whatever. If I get this big project finished by Friday, I get to go out for a drink and a good dinner on Friday night. You get the idea.

Punishments also affect behavior, but they are much weaker tools than rewards. For example, I have read about people who set a goal for themselves, with the threat that if they don't reach it, they have to send a substantial financial donation to an organization they loathe. Maybe this has worked for some people. Frankly, I cannot imagine myself doing it. In my opinion, based on both professional expertise and personal experience, rewards are the way to go.

Breaking down the task. Sometimes the challenge just seems too daunting. The goal is too far off and the path seems impossible. It becomes increasingly difficult to keep putting one foot in front of the other even though you really want to achieve the goal.

The trick here is to break the task down into small, manageable chunks. All you have to do right now is complete the first chunk—don't worry about the rest of it. That way you get to feel as if you are making progress. You may even want to create a visual graphic for yourself, like those giant thermometers that charitable organizations use to show the progress of their fundraising, or the image of a track on the treadmill screen that shows how far you have gone.

Remember Mariana (in chapter 3) and her three-year plan to get through her PhD program as fast as possible? She drew a ladder on a piece of paper and labeled each step with one of the hurdles she had to complete to earn her degree.

It looked something like figure 6.1. She deliberately drew the ladder from the bottom up, because it felt like a really hard climb.

And she kept that piece of paper on her desk for three years. Each time she completed a task she crossed it off. By breaking down the task into manageable chunks, she was able to keep herself intensely focused and achieve her goal.

My favorite example of using both of these tactics—rewards and breaking down the task—comes from my time in graduate school. The textbook for one of my classes was just awful—poorly written, very dense, boring as heck. My assignment was to read several chapters, and I was trying, unsuccessfully, to make myself slog through it. Finally, I pushed back from my desk and started yelling a few unprintable words. My husband asked me what was wrong and I told him I was never going to be able to read the assigned material. He wisely encouraged me to step away from my desk and take a break.

When I came back to the book a few minutes later, I finished the page I was on and turned to the next page. I found a note tucked into my book—"You're doing great, keep going!" I smiled, read the page, and when I turned the next one, there was another note—"Two pages down, you're on the way." I realized that my darling husband had tucked an encouraging note between each page of the remaining chapter. All I had to do was read one more page to get to the next note. I whizzed through the rest of the chapter and smiled much of the time.

Visualizing the goal. Sports psychologists who work with top athletes use visualization a lot (see https://www.llewellyn.com/encyclopedia/article/244). They teach athletes to improve their performance by visualizing themselves succeeding at a challenge. A basketball player mastering the skill of shooting a three-pointer learns to visualize the ball going into the basket. A champion ice-skater learns to visualize landing her triple-axel jump perfectly. (Aren't you impressed that I am using sports examples when I am totally not a sports enthusiast? I had to ask for my husband's help on the terminology. See, no one achieves greatness alone.)

When you are battling procrastination, you can use visualization of achievement and success as a way to keep yourself focused on completing your tasks with skill and determination.

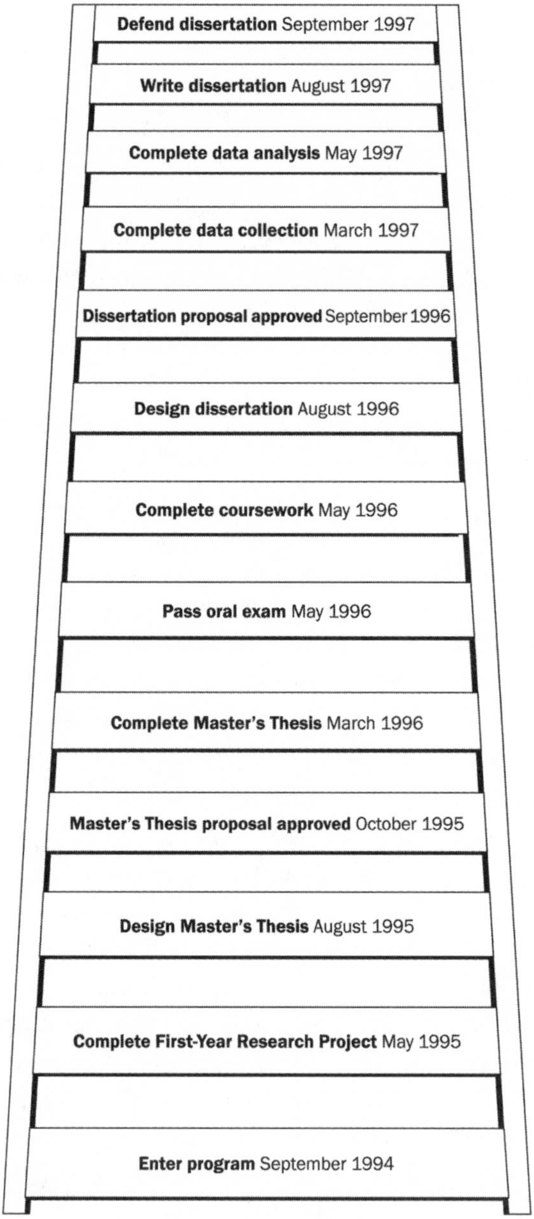

Figure 6.1. Breaking down a task. *Mary Clare Butler*

Making a public commitment. There's a ton of research that shows that telling others about your goal increases the likelihood you will persist at it.[2] It's one of the reasons that coaching works— because your coach will hold you accountable for the things you said you would do. Similarly, peer groups often provide a setting to make and keep your commitments. In the business world, CEO peer groups help business leaders learn from each other, find support, and also hold each other accountable for the actions they have promised to do. Whether you share your goal with just one close friend or you broadcast it to the world, making your commitment public will help you stay the course.

A good example of this is my writing this book. When I first started, it was a secret project. I didn't know if I could really do it and I wasn't sure I wanted to. So I wrote on my own and didn't tell anyone about it. But once I got serious about the project, I told all kinds of people. I already had a high level of intrinsic motivation, but telling my friends and my professional associates solidified my commitment. After all, I didn't want to look like a dilettante, in my own eyes or in theirs.

Developing routines or habits. Psychologists have developed a theory called "ego depletion." The theory proposes that people have a limited pool of resources we can use to control all the facets of our behavior. Every time we have to exercise self-control— make ourselves do something we don't really want to do, or stop doing something we enjoy—that pool of resources gets slightly smaller. Once the pool of resources is depleted entirely (high fatigue), it becomes much more difficult for us to control our behavior.

One way around this problem is to develop strong and productive habits or routines. For example, you get up and go to the gym every morning. You spend the first hour at work as a writing hour—no emails, chatting with friends, etc.—only writing. Once you have formed strong habits, you no longer have to draw from the pool of resources. You don't have to expend the energy to convince yourself to do the right thing and not that other thing you really want to do in the moment (such as stay in bed or spend your first hour at work playing video games). Developing strong habits makes your behavior more automatic, allowing you to save your energy, better control your decisions, and stay on task.

Social self-regulation. Victor Hugo was a famous writer in the eighteenth century who was both persistent and consistent in seeing his manuscripts all the way through to the end. He also very much enjoyed going to the pub and drinking with his friends, so much so that it sometimes interfered with his work. However, he was able to maintain his motivation even during tedious aspects of the writing process because he mastered the skill of "social self-regulation." For example, during times he needed to focus, he told his personal servant not to let him have his bar clothes until he finished his manuscript. Sure enough—he would complete the manuscript before going out to celebrate with his friends.[3]

Sadly, most of us do not have personal servants these days. But we can still use social self-regulation. I happen to have a ferocious sweet tooth. In fact, my husband calls it my "sweet tusk." Since I don't want to weigh three hundred pounds, I need to control my passion for chocolates. But I don't want to give them up altogether. When I buy a box of chocolates, I give them to my husband and tell him to hide them. When I ask for one, he is to give it to me, but only one a day. It actually works great. I get to enjoy my chocolate without going berserk and eating twelve of them.

Cultivating a learning goal (mastery) orientation. Psychologists have identified two different kinds of goals, learning goals and performance goals.[4] Learning goals are about the *journey*. For example, I want to master a new selling approach and apply it to my company's services. Or I want to understand how to be the kind of parent who inspires high achievement motivation in my children.

Performance goals are about the *destination*. I want to sell over a million dollars' worth of my company's product this year. I want my daughter to get into an Ivy League School.

Of course, you need to have both kinds of goals to be successful. But focusing mainly on performance goals can actually set you back. This is especially true when you are trying to acquire new skills and knowledge. Too much focus on the end goal makes you more likely to say "I'm just no good at this," rather than "I need to practice more." As a result, you become more susceptible to feeling discouraged and giving up. If instead you take a learning orientation, negative feedback becomes information. You'll focus more on discovering effective strategies to attain your goals. As a result, you are more likely to persist even when you're facing challenges and setbacks.

Interrupting counterproductive habits. A few paragraphs ago, I wrote about how building productive routines and habits makes you more efficient because they require less decision-making and therefore take less energy. Unfortunately, counterproductive habits work the same way. Because they are automatic, you're often not even aware that you're doing them, so the first step is building awareness. For example, while I've been working on this book, every time an email comes in, I tend to stop writing and read the email. This wastes a lot of time because most of the emails are unimportant. And even with the more important ones, by the time I have read them, decided what to do about them, perhaps responded, and then returned to my writing, I have usually lost track of my thought process and have to reread some of my work to get back on track. So this interferes with my productivity, and at the end of my writing time I get frustrated because I didn't get as much done as I had hoped. If I don't watch out, I'll get discouraged and start procrastinating or give up on my project altogether.

Once you become aware of a counterproductive habit, the solution is to interrupt it in some way. For example, I could do my writing on a computer that doesn't have internet access, or turn off the email notifications. Or I could shout, "NO!" to myself when I am tempted to check my email. The point is to interfere with the automatic nature of the behavior, so you can take control over it.

As you can see, there are a number of effective tactics you can use to tackle a procrastination problem. But I want to add a final note about procrastination. Much of the time it is one of the ways we sabotage ourselves, and to achieve greatness we need to find a way to overcome our lazy, avoidant tendencies. But sometimes, procrastination gives us important information. Here's an example.

A couple of years ago I decided to write a book. I thought about a topic that would be good for marketing my business, I wrote an outline, and I hired a researcher to help me investigate the topic. Four months later I had written *not one word*. I kept trying to make myself work on the book and I just wasn't doing it.

I'm usually a pretty disciplined, focused person, so this was unusual for me. As I reflected on what was going on, I realized—*I was trying to write the wrong book*. It was the book I felt I *should* write, not the one I cared about. In a flash I recognized that what I really wanted to write was an entirely different book—this one. Is this book going to be good for my business? I don't know. But I am writing energetically and thinking about the book all the time. This is the book I was meant to write.

I could have used all the anti-procrastination tactics in the world and I probably would never have written that other book. If I had written it, it would almost certainly have been worse than mediocre. Sometimes procrastination tells you that you are trying to make yourself do the wrong thing.

Once again, those childhood "laws" can mislead us. Just like "Always do your best" is a terrible trap, so is "Don't be a quitter." Doing your best and being persistent are really important elements of your character. But sometimes, *quitting something you really dislike and are never going to be good at is a really good idea*.

Another way to think about this is to calibrate the degree of pain you are experiencing. If you're comfortable, that's great— nothing wrong with comfort as far as I'm concerned. But sometimes to achieve your greatness, you have to push out of your comfort zone. You have to do things that are difficult, scary, painful, frustrating, or embarrassing. If you never leave your comfort zone, you probably won't achieve your greatness.

Going to business school was like that for me. I was very comfortable in my psychology niche. I was a respected expert. I could talk about my field with confidence. I spent my time with colleagues who saw the world much the same way I did. When I decided to go to business school, the prospect was daunting. I would be in classes with people who were already seasoned business leaders. I was the only psychologist in the class. Eighty percent of my fellow students were male, and most of them were younger than me. I'd be taking courses in finance, accounting, marketing, global strategy—all sorts of things I knew nothing about.

I tried to prepare myself by reading some basic business textbooks, but when I walked into my first class I was really intimidated. Besides the fact that my classmates knew much more about business than I did, they were almost all "Type-A" personalities. (Type-A people are described as competitive, aggressive, ambitious, impatient, highly organized, and time-conscious.) In most small-group settings, a natural leader quickly emerges and takes charge. In business school, almost everyone was one of those natural leaders. It was amusing to watch us (me included) jostling for position. Talk about uncomfortable—I felt like a total fish out of water.

In time I found my place in the group and my two years in business school were exciting and fun. But I didn't know that going in. Had I allowed myself to be swayed by my discomfort, I would never have been able to pursue this career that has brought me great satisfaction.

But if you are in agony zone, you may have set yourself the wrong goal. You are aiming for a goal that is not you. You don't have the talent, or you don't have the resources, or you don't have the passion. Most often that happens when you are trying to achieve someone else's vision of greatness for you, not your own. We are especially vulnerable to this risk when it's our parents' dreams we are trying to fulfill. We'll talk about how to avoid this in chapter 8.

There's an interesting new theory in psychology called *Broaden and Build*.[5] Linking psychological research with evolutionary theory, Broaden and Build proposes that when people experience

positive emotions, they think more broadly and freely and generate better solutions. This has evolutionary implications, because
better solutions to life's challenges increase your chances of survival. Broaden and Build provides broad research and theoretical
support for the notion that experiencing positive feelings, not agony, will enable you to achieve your goals more effectively.

And now for a delightful tidbit. In 2019 the American Psychological Association decided to sponsor a video contest called *Psyc-
Shorts.* The goal was to produce a two-minute video on an important piece of psychological research, designed for a lay audience.
My research advisor (and nephew), Simon Golden, recommended
that we do a video on Broaden and Build. With the help of Yellow-
box, a cutting-edge marketing agency, we produced a video,
Broaden and Build: The Tale of Palimbo, and we won one of the
top prizes. (If you want to see the video, check out https://www.
apa.org/news/apa/2019/psycshorts-contest-winners.)

I want to close this chapter with two of my favorite examples of
people who have lived their greatness. The first one comes from
my son, Josh, who told me about a trip he took to a ski town in
northern Japan. There he had the opportunity to observe a man
making soba noodles by hand. He watched in fascination as this
man went about mixing and rolling dough, then cutting the noodles with a special knife, one noodle at a time. He produced perfect noodles with great concentration, consistency, and skill, day
after day. This man is not a renowned celebrity in Japan or even in
his town. He is just a great noodle maker.

The second example is the Watts Towers in Los Angeles. The
first time you see them you cannot believe your eyes. You're driving through one of the bleakest urban ghettos in America, the
Watts neighborhood of LA, and there against the horizon is a
collection of fantastic metal structures. They seem completely out
of place and otherworldly. And then, as you draw near, you discover that they are totally covered with the wildest mosaics. Take a
look at figure 6.2. What the heck is going on here?

The Watts Towers are the largest work of art on the planet that
was built by one person, alone. That person was Simon Rodia, a

Figure 6.2. The Watts Towers. © *iStock / Getty Images Plus / Joe_Potato*

tiny, illiterate Italian immigrant who worked in construction. In 1921, Rodia decided he wanted to "do something big." He bought a small lot in Watts near the train station so people could see his work. And for the next thirty-three years he spent every moment of his free time building the Towers. He used no scaffolding, no power tools, no welding, and no bolts.

The Watts Towers are challenging on several levels. Let's face it—what kind of a nut spends thirty-three years of his life building something bizarre and useless? Yet, on the other hand, what a magnificent achievement! Rodia wanted to do something big, and by golly, he did it. The Towers are breathtakingly beautiful and many people find them spiritually inspiring. They are the embodiment of passion and individuality, and once you have seen them it is hard to stop thinking about them.

Rodia also challenges our notions of who is an artist. He had no education and no artistic training. He was a poor tile setter who made use of scrap materials to build something enormous and utterly unique. He may have been influenced by festival towers he saw in Italian villages, but what he built was quite different. Where did that vision come from?

The Watts Towers show us what passion and vision and thinking big and persistence and focus and, yes, obsession can accomplish. How many of us long for some of that passion in our lives? For the opportunity to make something marvelous happen? To leave a unique and beautiful legacy? Perhaps we need to spend more time discovering our inner Simon Rodia.

Next time you are in Los Angeles, go and see the Watts Towers. They will change you.

One final note: your greatness will probably change over your lifespan. What you choose to be great at when you're twenty-five and when you're seventy-five are likely to be quite different. So you're almost certainly going to have to revisit this process of choosing and living your greatness again and again. We'll talk a lot more about that in chapter 9.

The ultimate goal of curating your life is to choose your own greatness and then go for it. Whether it's helping a troubled child, making amazing noodles, or becoming an inspiring corporate executive, find it and pursue it. It's what your energy is for.

KEY TAKEAWAYS

- Greatness requires three ingredients: talent, opportunity, and fierce dedication. You don't have control over your talents and not much control over your opportunities. But you do have control over what you choose to dedicate yourself to.
- Consider:

  - What kind of effort will this work require?
  - What do I have to learn?
  - How will I stay great?"
  - What tools do I need?
  - What support do I need?
  - How do I measure greatness?

- People rarely become great all by themselves.
- To enhance motivation, use:

  - rewards and punishments;
  - breaking down the task;
  - visualizing the goal;
  - making a public commitment;
  - developing routines or habits;
  - social self-regulation;
  - cultivating a learning goal (mastery) orientation;
  - interrupting counterproductive habits.

- Sometimes procrastination tells you that you are trying to make yourself do the wrong thing.
- If you never leave your comfort zone, you probably won't achieve your greatness.

7

CURATE YOUR WORKPLACE

So far, this book has been about you—about how you can curate your life to maximize your productivity and your joy. Although I have talked about curation in the context of relationships, the emphasis has been on how you, as an individual, can make choices that will lead to greatness—or not. But if I am not careful, I am going to lead you into a trap. Because as I've already said, many of us, especially Americans, really like to believe that each person is in charge of his or her own destiny. As a result, we tend to attribute success and failure to individual characteristics, rather than recognizing the enormous power of the context in which we live and work.

I'll give you a personal example. I am a goal-driven, hardworking person. I value my energy, my focus, and my high standards. I firmly believe that when I am being paid to work, I am ethically obligated to provide the best-quality service I can. I have lived up to those expectations in every job I have held, from being a camp counselor to waitressing to teaching to running Gail Golden Consulting. Every job—except one.

I had to work to help pay my expenses when I was a college student. So I was pleased to get a part-time job working in a library. I love books, I enjoy putting things in order, I'm good at serving customers—it seemed like a great fit. In my first few days on the job I was given a number of menial jobs to do. For example, I was given a long list of numbers and told to copy them by hand onto another list. It seemed very inefficient to me, but hey, if that's what the boss wanted me to do, that's what I would do.

Most of the people who worked in the library were full-time library professionals, not part-time student workers. They watched me working away and seemed to be a little amused. Over the next few weeks, I gradually realized something odd. Most of the time, I was the only person doing any work in the library. The others would read the newspaper, drink coffee, and chat amiably. I remember one time one of the women offered to read my palm. It was a pleasant, relaxed environment, and nobody was working except me.

I would love to tell you that I kept working away, holding myself to my high ethical standard of providing value in order to earn my paycheck. But that would be a big lie. The truth is that within a month I had settled into the library culture of sitting around, chatting, and drinking coffee. I felt vaguely uneasy about what I was doing, but I no longer did much work. Why bother?

A year after I had left that job for a more interesting one, the library was moved into a different space. A friend of mine was part of the crew who moved the books, and he told me that he and his coworkers had never seen such chaos. Hundreds of books were missing, and the rest were mostly misfiled. It was a wonder that any client ever found anything useful in that library. I was a little embarrassed that I had been part of the team that had done such a lousy job. What had happened to me when I worked there? Where had Gail Hartmann (my name then) gone?

The fact is that context has a huge impact on how we act. It's not that we're robots who can be programmed by others—of course we have choices about how we will behave. But if you believe you will always act the same regardless of your environment, you are almost certainly kidding yourself. The people and situations around us can bring out remarkable acts of bravery and goodness—or they can turn us into lazy slobs.

I've mentioned Malcolm Gladwell's book *Outliers* earlier.[1] It's an investigation into what makes people extraordinary. In the book, Gladwell focuses on resources and opportunities—for example, when and where you were born, the financial and educational resources available to you, and so on. He found that circumstances played a huge role in who became an outlier.

What I'm talking about now is a little different. Even in a situation where you have the opportunity and the resources to be great, sometimes *context* gets in the way. There was no resource constraint that prevented me from being a terrific library assistant. But the culture of laziness was so strong, it was almost impossible to resist.

Which brings us to what it means to be a leader. These days we often talk as if everyone is a leader, which I don't find very useful. In this chapter I'm using the word to mean anyone who is responsible for managing the work of others. Leadership can include selecting people for specific tasks, showing them how to do the work, providing feedback and evaluation, choosing who will be rewarded and how, and deciding about retention, promotion, and termination. Being a leader also involves being a role model, providing inspiration to others, and creating the culture of the workplace.

I'm not trying to teach you about leadership in general. But I do think it's important for leaders to think about curation, not only for themselves but for their people as well. When you are a leader, your team looks to you for guidance about how to work, perhaps much more so than you realize.

There's a famous story about a company I once consulted to. It was Friday afternoon at about 5:30 and the elevator heading down from the upper floors was filled with people. It stopped at the fifth floor, the executive suite, and the CEO of the company got on. As the elevator was descending, he glanced at his watch. When the doors opened on the first floor, the CEO got out—but no one else did. They all rode back up to their offices.

Why? When they saw the CEO glance at his watch, they assumed he was thinking, "Ah ha! I see my people are not very hard workers—they're all heading home instead of staying in the office late to ensure the work gets done." No one wanted to be seen as a slacker, so they all went back upstairs. The truth was that the CEO had a plane to catch and was checking to make sure he would make his flight.

I'm not telling this story in order to put blame on the CEO. He didn't know that the others had misinterpreted his gesture. One of the realities of being a senior executive is that you are highly visible. People watch and interpret everything you do. As a leader, you need to be aware that others are constantly watching you for signals on how to play the game. So it makes sense to be intentional and consistent about the messages you are sending.

That means that beyond curating your own life, *you have to think about how to create an environment where your people are encouraged and supported to curate theirs*. As I have said from the start, this is not about being touchy-feely. Curation is a key element in getting the best performance from your people, both because they are using their energy in a focused and efficient manner and because they are finding meaning and joy in what they are doing.

Leading for curation affects many aspects of leadership. One aspect is *Energy Curation*, which is similar to what I've been talking about all through this book. Energy Curation means that leaders have to design a culture that encourages people to use their energy optimally—to take regular breaks, to take good care of themselves, and to focus on the tasks that are most important. Leaders must not only talk about Energy Curation—they must also model it, and most important, reward it.

I often hear complaints from my clients that their manager sends them emails in the middle of the night or on the weekend. As far as I'm concerned, the manager has the right to work whenever she or he wants to. If you're a night person, feel free to attack your email at 2:00 a.m. But be mindful of the messages you're sending, both the literal messages and the symbolic ones. To your team, your timing may imply that you expect them to be "on" all the time.

They may be right about that—in which case, shame on you. That expectation will lead first to inefficiency and lowered quality of work and then to burnout. Your people will be less engaged. Your turnover rates will rise. The costs of medical care for your people will skyrocket. This is not a pretty picture.

Believe me, I am a strong believer in high expectations for employees, both for quantity and quality of work. Many of the leaders I work with are frustrated by their perception that their people are not as committed to peak performance as they want them to be. The happiest workplaces I have worked in or observed are companies with high, clear expectations for commitment and performance. But you're not going to get better performance by sending out the message that people should work 24/7. Au contraire!

There's another problem with the 2:00 a.m. emails—sleep disruption. Ariana Huffington has written extensively on the importance of sleep. A few years ago, she exhausted herself into a major medical crisis, and since then she has become a spokesperson for healthy sleep habits.[2] Your midnight messaging will not be promoting healthy sleep habits in your team members—so knock it off. (An aside—I heard Huffington speak on this topic a few years ago at a large conference for women. She was an eloquent and compelling speaker. And she brought the house down when she concluded, "So remember, ladies, you're going to sleep your way to the top.")

But wait—what if you get a great idea on Sunday at 6:30 a.m. and you really want to share it with one of your people? Fortunately, Outlook has provided a wonderful tool called "Delay Delivery." You can draft your email, set a reasonable Monday-morning delivery time, and give both yourself and your employee some peace.

Another aspect of Energy Curation is limiting the sheer number of priorities you give to your team. Sometimes the most energetic and creative leaders are terrible at this. Saul was a good example. At least once a week he would get excited about a new idea. He was an avid reader and an innovative thinker, so he would often get fascinated by how his team could apply some new approach to their business. He would hold a meeting to share his initiative and set a group of people to work to explore it.

That was all fine, except for one thing. He never remembered to follow up with his team members to say, "You know that Jumping Bean initiative we started on last month? I'm killing it off—it's not the way we're going to go." He just kept piling more and more on, like that overloaded stove top I described in chapter 1.

Saul's team loved him—he was an exciting leader to work for—and they prided themselves on their ability to keep up with him. But his racing to bring in new ideas without eliminating some of the old ones was starting to burn his team out. Fortunately, he realized what was happening and began to hold "Liberation Parties" where projects were killed off. And his team became more productive than ever.

Balancing high expectations for excellence with a thoughtful understanding of Energy Curation is a major challenge for many leaders. Some years ago, I was asked to assess Michelle, a very talented young woman who was being considered for a major promotion. She was highly qualified for the position, with strong skills both technically and interpersonally. I was pleased to recommend her for the promotion. But in my assessment report, one of my observations was that her strong drive for success sometimes led her to overestimate what was realistic. This caused her to become frustrated or impatient with the pace of a project. I recommended that she work on understanding and leveraging the individual style and pace of each member of her team so she could continue to produce outstanding results in a sustainable manner—in other words, not burn herself or her people out.

The good news was that Michelle got the promotion and I had the opportunity to coach her during the first few months. She took my recommendation to heart and worked hard to become a more flexible leader, even as she continued to push herself and her team for peak performance. She performed really well in her new role and went on to further promotions and successes.

As I said earlier, leaders have to *talk* about Energy Curation, *model* it, and *reward* it. Some leaders recognize that their responsibility goes even further. It's not enough to limit your demands on your people. Sometimes you have to intervene in the demands they are setting on themselves. My favorite story about this kind of leadership comes from my father's history.

My father, Walter Hartmann, escaped from Nazi Germany in 1939 on the Kindertransport—the remarkable humanitarian initiative by Great Britain to get Jewish children out of Germany and into England. He lived through World War II in England, working at a variety of jobs. At the end of the war, when the concentration camps were liberated, many children who had been incarcerated in the camps were brought to England to be rehabilitated, psychologically and physically. The rehab centers needed staff who spoke German, Yiddish, or Polish, and my father stepped forward to work at Windermere, one of those centers.

I'm sure you can imagine how incredibly hard that work was. These were children who had been shattered by the losses and horrors they had witnessed. My father later became a psychologist, but at that time he had no training for this kind of work. As a Holocaust survivor himself, who had lost both of his parents to the genocide, the work must have triggered his own losses and traumas. He and the other staff did their best, but the work was emotionally exhausting.

Every week they got one day off. And the leader of Windermere established a surprising policy. On their day off, staff members were *not permitted* to be at the center. That's right—they weren't just encouraged to take a break; they were *required* to. The leader knew that they were so committed to the children they were serving that they would work themselves into the ground unless he prevented it.

Fortunately, very few people have jobs that are as emotionally devastating as working with children who are concentration camp survivors. Nonetheless, many people invest a lot of emotional energy in their work, and sometimes it is the job of the leader to insist that they observe boundaries that they otherwise might ignore.

A boss (or an author!) who tells you that you have to take time off—that may seem patronizing to you. But part of a manager's job is to help create the environment that enables his or her team to do their best work. And sometimes that means telling them to go home.

To summarize, leading for curation means, first of all, helping your people manage their energy wisely. That includes:

- being a good role model in your own work style
- setting reasonable expectations for how much time people have to be "on"
- sometimes protecting your people from their unreasonable expectations of themselves

A second focus for leading for curation is *Risk Curation*. Almost every company I work with emphasizes the importance of creativity and innovation. In today's fast-paced environment, the agility to try out new ideas and make changes quickly is a crucial capability. In order to have that kind of agility, Risk Curation is essential.

I'll give you an example of how *not* to do it. Some years ago, I witnessed a sad scene of a misguided attempt to foster innovation and creativity. My client, Jeff, was the CEO of a health care company. He had invited me to attend a meeting of his team of C-suite executives so I could observe his leadership style and how his team interacted. Jeff's natural leadership style was very domineering and even aggressive. He and I had been working on the coaching goal of helping him to become a more approachable, collaborative leader, so I was looking forward to seeing him in action. As we were walking into the meeting, he told me his main objective for this meeting was to encourage his team members to bring him bolder, more innovative ideas for how to transform their business.

Jeff exchanged a few pleasantries with his team and then outlined his agenda. "I want to go around the table and ask each of you to share a new idea you have for our company. We can discuss the ideas and decide which ones we want to move forward. I'll start." He then described his own thoughts about new directions for the company. When he was finished, he called on each team member in turn, and each person said something like, "Wow, Jeff, I think your ideas are the greatest. I think we should hop on those right away."

Needless to say, Jeff was very disappointed in the meeting. We debriefed afterward, and I was able to help him see where he had gone wrong. First of all, he had made the tactical error of starting with his own ideas rather than inviting the others to speak first. Of course, they were going to endorse what the boss suggested! But more importantly, because there was a climate of fear on his team, no one was willing to risk sharing his or her ideas only to have Jeff dismiss them. The good news is that over the next year I was able to help Jeff shift his style to be more encouraging of his team members, and as the team climate changed people were willing to share their new ideas more frequently.

One of the biggest barriers to innovation is fear. Tom Yorton is the former CEO of Second City Works, the business-to-business arm of the brilliant improv troupe in Chicago that has dominated the American comedy scene for many years. Yorton, along with coauthor Kelly Leonard, wrote an influential book about stimulating innovation and creativity titled *Yes, And*.[3] I heard Yorton speak on a panel shortly after I became a leadership consultant in 2003 and I remember his presentation vividly. He talked about how most workplaces are strangled by fear. People are terrified to make mistakes, so they play it safe. In other words, the context teaches them that all mistakes are equally important—that a minor typo on an internal document matters as much as an architectural design flaw that results in the deaths of many people.

In my language, that's an absence of Risk Curation. The leaders are failing to help people differentiate between what is critically important—where greatness lies for them and the organization—and what is only moderately important or not important at all.

This kind of work environment was beautifully described by Joseph Heller in his novel, *Something Happened:*

> In the office in which I work there are five people of whom I am afraid. Each of these five people is afraid of four people (excluding overlaps), for a total of twenty, and each of these twenty people is afraid of six people, making a total of one hundred and twenty people who are feared by at least one other person. Each of these one hundred and twenty people is afraid of the other one hundred and nineteen, and all of these one hundred and forty-five people are afraid of the twelve men at the top who helped found and build the company and now own and direct it. . . .
>
> I have a feeling that someone nearby is soon going to find out something about me that will mean the end, although I can't imagine what that something is. . . .
>
> In my department, there are six people who are afraid of me, and one small secretary who is afraid of all of us. I have one other person working for me who is not afraid of anyone, not even me, and I would fire him quickly, but I'm afraid of him. [4]

Heller wrote his book over forty-five years ago, but it still describes many of the companies I have worked with. The good news is there are ways to change that culture, some of which are outlined in Leonard and Yorton's book. They propose a radical idea—that powerful tactics to reduce fear and liberate innovation in the corporate world can be found in exercises that were developed for improvisational theater. Now that's not obvious, at least not for me. As a business leader, I don't really want my team acting like the characters played by John Belushi or Tina Fey or Stephen Colbert.

But Leonard and Yorton make a powerful case for their approach. For example, there is the "Yes, and" communication technique that is the title of their book. Most business leaders are highly educated, and most highly educated people have a *lot* of training in critical thinking. You put an idea in front of me and I can usually find the seventeen things wrong with it in very short order. And that's what business leaders commonly do. The result—people don't bring them ideas because they know they will be shot down.

But leaders have a choice. Instead of responding with, "No, because . . ." or "Yes, but . . ." we can listen to someone's idea and respond with "Yes, and . . . ." Here's an example. A young consultant, Martha, was just starting out at a consulting firm—let's call it Acme Consulting. She had a manager who was good at "Yes, and." One day Martha walked into his office with a new idea. Sitting on an airplane, she had met Linda, a senior executive in a global professional services firm. They each talked about their work. It turned out that Linda's company really needed some of the services that Acme could offer. And Acme could really benefit from some of the offerings Linda's company provided. By the time the plane landed, the two women had hatched a plot to create an exchange of services between their two companies.

Acme had never done something like this before, but Martha was convinced it was a great idea. She certainly did not have the clout to make the project happen by herself, so she took the idea to her manager. He could have shut it down immediately. Instead he said, "Yes, great idea. And I'd like you to introduce me to Linda so the three of us can sketch out what this might look like. Then I can take the idea to the Acme leadership team and see what they say." So they worked together to come up with a plan, and eventually they were able to set up an exchange of services that proved to be useful to both companies.

Working for a "Yes, and" leader is energizing. It enables people who are lower on the food chain to bring their ideas to the leadership team without fear of humiliation. Look, I know that most innovative suggestions are never going to become reality. Everyone cites that famous anecdote about how Thomas Edison and his team tried out three thousand different designs for the electric lightbulb before they found the one that worked. But if Thomas Edison had worked for a boss who was a squelch, who knows—we might still be reading by candlelight! Part of a leader's job is to help sort out the great ideas from the not-so-great ones. But if leaders aren't open to at least some of their people's innovative ideas, their companies will be left behind. To use a current cliché, leaders who excel at innovation help their people "fail fast and fail often."

Risk Curating leaders know how to identify mistakes and potential mistakes that are unacceptable, because they threaten the well-being of the company and its customers. But they also help their people to identify the acceptable mistakes, the ones that either don't matter that much or that have the potential to lead to something great. Then people are not so afraid, so they take reasonable chances, they unleash their creativity, and great things can happen.

To summarize, the second part of leading for curation, Risk Curation, is about helping your people differentiate between the mission critical work where a cautious approach is wise and the other aspects of work where mistakes can be made and risks can be taken. No leader will be able to eliminate fear from the workplace entirely. I actually don't think you would want to. A little fear can be motivating and help people remember where the boundaries lie. But in general, reducing fear leads to new levels of innovation and success.

Break time. Think about your work environment. Is it one that makes it easy for you to take a few minutes? Can you get outdoors? Do you get in trouble if you look as if you're not working? Maybe you need to take a sneaky break? Going to the bathroom might work. Do whatever it takes to refresh your body and your mind. And if you're working in a place that doesn't make it easy to take breaks, maybe you can figure out what to do about that.

The third part of leading for curation is *Recognition Curation*. I mentioned back in chapter 6 that one of the most powerful ways to influence other people's behavior is to reward them when they do what you want. But you need to be careful. It's easy to inadvertently reward behaviors that you don't want. How often have you watched a parent giving all kinds of attention to a child having a temper tantrum? Even if it's negative attention, it's rewarding the child's behavior. The same thing can happen in the workplace. So Recognition Curation means getting very clear on what greatness looks like in your work setting and then rewarding the behaviors that demonstrate that greatness.

Here's a good example. I worked for some years as a clinical psychologist in a medical center. The medical director was a renowned physician, a tall, brilliant Scot whom we all admired immensely. Dr. McSherry was a very busy leader with a broad scope of responsibility. But every once in a while, when I was giving a presentation to the medical residents, I would see him standing at the back of the room, listening. And sometimes, within a day or two, I'd get a handwritten note from Dr. McSherry praising my work.

Those notes meant the world to me. Dr. McSherry didn't send them all the time, just when he thought something was outstanding. They inspired me to do my best, and they affirmed that I was doing great work. It's been twenty years since I left the medical center and Dr. McSherry has passed away. But I still have those notes.

Some readers may be appalled by what I just wrote. You may be thinking, "Really? Along with all my other leadership responsibilities, I have to take time out to write friggin' thank you notes? My people are getting paid, for goodness sake! Isn't that enough?" My answer is, no, it's not enough—not if you want greatness. You don't have to write thank you notes if that's not your thing. But having some way to personally acknowledge and reward outstanding work—that's a tool you should have in your leadership tool kit.

You also don't have to do it all the time—in fact, you shouldn't. Back in chapter 6 I alluded to reinforcement schedules. I'm not going to go into all the technical details, but we know that the frequency and predictability of rewards very much influences their effectiveness. Dr. McSherry's notes were so powerful in part because they were rare and unexpected. So do an experiment—

find a way to occasionally reward great work and observe what happens.

However, there's another problem. It's not always easy for a senior leader to know who's great and who isn't. Some people are very talented at creating the illusion of greatness. I once participated in a project team with five of my colleagues. It was a good team and we worked well together. There were two team members who were well known to others in the organization. Tim was kind of a goofball. He had trouble sitting still, he cracked a lot of jokes, and he often made fun of himself. Meanwhile, Lawrence was widely admired for his poise and executive presence. A handsome man, he didn't say much, but when he spoke others tended to listen.

Colleagues who were working on other teams told me how lucky we were to have Lawrence on our team. But they commiserated with us for having to put up with Tim. Meanwhile, those of us on the team knew the real story. Lawrence was an "empty suit," a guy who made a good impression but actually contributed very little to the work. Meanwhile, Tim was a genius project manager who kept us all on track. We would never have completed our work on time without Tim's guidance.

As I said, it's not always easy to determine who is actually doing great work. It's important for senior leaders to gather data from other sources, rather than relying purely on their own impressions of who is making the greatest contributions.

It's also your responsibility as an employee to make your greatness visible to your leaders. I'm not talking about being a show-off or a braggart. But you can make it easier for your manager to recognize your greatness if you give him or her a line of sight to what you are accomplishing. This is part of what coaches often call "managing up." Some people are very uneasy with that term because it implies "sucking up." But that's not what I'm talking about. Good leaders want to know what their people are doing. They want to hear about successes and breakthroughs and great accomplishments. So it makes sense to tell them.

If you work for a company that still has annual or semiannual performance reviews, that's a good time to catalog your achievements for your manager. But in between, it's often a good idea to find low-key ways to stay on your boss's radar. Maybe you can poke your head into his or her office to share good news about something you've accomplished. Maybe you can copy him or her on an email announcing a success.

For my clients I created a little chart that I call the "radar grid." Take a look at Figure 7.1.

There are two ways you can be on your boss's radar. Visibility is what I've just been talking about—you help your boss to know how you are making a contribution to the company. Maintenance is when there is negative "buzz" around you, when your boss hears

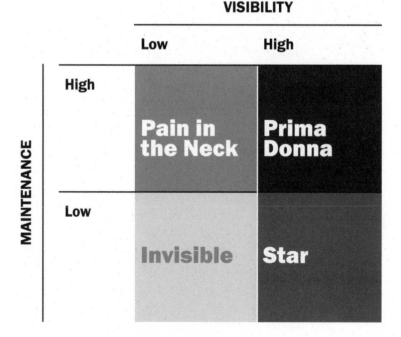

Figure 7.1. The radar grid. *Mary Clare Butler*

you are irritating others and making the workplace less pleasant. There are four quadrants in the grid:

- Low visibility/Low maintenance—This is when your boss doesn't see or hear much about you. You're not a problem, but you're not noteworthy either. This is often a formula for getting stuck in the same job.
- Low visibility/High maintenance—This is when most or all of what your boss hears about you is that you're difficult to work with. It's a good formula for getting terminated.
- High visibility/High maintenance—This is when your boss can clearly see the value you are bringing to the company, but it comes at a cost in interpersonal friction. In this case, your boss will probably make a determination as to whether your value is so great that others will put up with your nonsense. In the current business climate, there is less and less tolerance for people who make trouble in the workplace. Increasing numbers of companies have installed a "No Jerks" rule and are enforcing it. If you're in this box, you're walking a tightrope. And you're likely to be sent to me for coaching.
- High visibility/Low maintenance—This is the magic formula, when your boss sees your contributions and doesn't have to worry about problems you are creating. This is the formula that often leads to promotions, raises, and other good outcomes.

In my coaching practice I see very few people who are in the "Pain in the Neck" box. Companies don't usually invest in coaching for those people. Some of my clients are in the "Invisible" box, where they need to work on how to demonstrate their value to the company more clearly so they slide over to the "Star" box. Others are in the "Prima Donna" box, where they need to work on reducing the level of maintenance they require so they drop down into the "Star" Box. And many of my clients are already Stars.

The point is that you can't just be *doing* great work; you have to be *seen* to be doing great work. Many women have particular trouble with this. They are performing wonders in the workplace but they don't know how to show their successes to their managers. This is partly because many workplaces put women in a double bind. If you don't talk about your successes, you get passed over. If you do, you're seen as a pushy, bossy, a show-off, whatever. If you're struggling with this challenge, a great book to read is *Breaking Through Bias* by Andrea Kramer and Alton Harris.[5] They provide some powerful and wise advice for women who are navigating their careers in male-dominated settings.

The point of managing up is to help your leader curate recognition for you appropriately. Don't expect him or her to do all the work to make this happen—find ways to get on that "visibility radar."

Recognition Curation is the mutual responsibility of the manager and the employee. With the right systems and attitudes in place, managers have a much better ability to determine who is doing great work on the mission-critical projects and provide appropriate rewards.

A fascinating new development in the arena of Recognition Curation is the rise of People Analytics. Companies are rapidly becoming more sophisticated in their use of technology to gather and analyze data about employee behavior. In addition to reviewing the content of emails, many companies are analyzing numerous other measures of employee productivity, such as:

- analyzing who emails whom and how quickly people respond;
- tracking how employees move throughout the building;
- recording and analyzing participation in meetings, including who speaks, whether others respond to their contribution, tone of voice, and so on.

There is certainly a spooky, "Big Brother" quality to some of these tools. There are ethical considerations about how companies employ them and whether they inform employees about what kinds of surveillance they are under. But People Analytics tools are here now, and will undoubtedly continue to be used and refined. And like any other powerful tools, they can be used for both positive and negative goals. When employed in a thoughtful and ethical manner, People Analytics can help to combat bias in the workplace and provide leaders with broader, more reliable data to inform their Recognition Curation.

As a cautionary tale, I want to provide an example of a workplace where not only was greatness unrecognized, it was actively discouraged. Alex was an executive in a professional services firm, reporting directly to the CEO. He was a highly experienced, whip-smart leader. He worked like a demon and had high expectations for his team members. He was invested in their development and they were devoted to him—except for one person, Elizabeth. Elizabeth was originally a consultant and had gained the attention and respect of the CEO. So he brought her into the organization, reporting to Alex.

Disaster ensued. Elizabeth saw herself as a favorite of the CEO and cultivated that relationship. She actively undermined Alex's authority. Alex confronted Elizabeth about her behavior, but Elizabeth ignored him and continued to focus on currying favor with the CEO. Over time, it worked. Alex's scope of responsibility was narrowed and his ability to provide his highly professional leadership to the firm was curtailed. Although he continued to enjoy the respect of others in the firm, the CEO no longer listened to his input. He excluded Alex from key meetings, gave him low-level tasks, and criticized him in front of other senior leaders.

Alex tried for several years to continue to provide top value to the firm, but his ability to do so was more and more constrained. Eventually he left for another leadership role, where he was able to deploy his considerable talents. When the CEO stepped down a year later, his successor quickly recognized that Elizabeth was a liability, but by then the damage had been done and the firm's finances were suffering.

What went wrong here? Three people played a part. Alex didn't do a great job of demonstrating his value to his boss. When he recognized that Elizabeth was undermining him, he didn't know how to respond in a powerful, effective manner. Elizabeth was so focused on promoting herself that she failed to build a strong alliance with Alex. Together, the two of them could have built a powerful enterprise, instead of battling with each other. And the CEO was blinded by Elizabeth's flattery and self-promotion and didn't do his due diligence to determine who was really providing value to the firm.

If you find yourself working in a setting that doesn't allow for or support greatness, get out if you possibly can. Your personal brand may be damaged by your association with such a company. And your joy, your pride, and your satisfaction in your work will seep away. Don't let that happen to you.

One of the really challenging parts of leading a curated team is Conflict Curation—making choices about when you will engage in conflict. Some people really enjoy a good fight, but for many of us engaging in battle is an enormous energy drain. Those of us who love fighting are at risk of initiating conflicts about relatively unimportant issues. Those of us who find conflict exhausting and unpleasant are likely to avoid conflicts about issues that really need to be addressed.

Consider my client Amanda. She was a senior leader in her company, highly respected for her ability to solve complex problems and get the job done. But her career was stalling because some of her colleagues found her difficult to work with. The reason? Once she was convinced that a certain path was the right one, she would fight endlessly for her point of view. That's admirable when you're fighting for an important issue—something that will really make a difference to the success of the company. But Amanda would put just as much energy into battling over small details. Her combativeness was exhausting her energy and was tiring out her colleagues as well. She needed to learn how to discriminate between battles that deserved to be fought and those to let go. She worked hard on that in her coaching and was delighted when she was promoted to a C-suite role a few months later.

The fifth and final aspect of leading a curated team is *Self-Awareness*. When I first made the shift from clinical to consulting psychology, many of my new colleagues believed that self-awareness was one of the most important qualities of a great leader. I was skeptical. It seemed a little squishy to me, compared with other, more observable qualities such as executive presence, strategic thinking, influencing without authority, and other well-known leadership attributes.

Fifteen-plus years later, my attitude has changed. Time and again I have observed how crucially important self-awareness is to leadership effectiveness. The ability to look fearlessly at yourself, to listen with receptivity to feedback from others who know you, and to utilize that information to develop and grow as a leader and a person—that's the stuff that great leaders are made of.

So what's that got to do with curation? Self-awareness enables leaders and potential leaders to focus their talents on what they are good at, instead of trying to be everything to everybody. Remember back in chapter 2? It was all about figuring out who you are and what really matters to you. Too often, leaders accept roles that are a really bad fit for them and then do them poorly.

Patrick is a good example. He was a brilliant residential interior designer. He understood how to help people create homes that they loved, homes that enabled them to live the lives they wanted to lead. He had deep technical knowledge of architecture and construction, building materials, history, and art. He also knew how to really listen to his clients so that he created spaces that were right for them, not some generic design that happened to be the latest trend.

Patrick was so good at what he did that his business grew rapidly. In order to keep up with the demand, he had to assemble a team to help manage all the aspects of a successful business—finance, accounting, sales, customer relations, supply chain, marketing, and so on.

Here's the problem. Patrick was a pretty awful people manager. Although he was a caring person who tried hard to be a good leader, the people who worked for him found him to be a very difficult boss. He was often inaccessible because he was concentrating on his creative work. He could be moody and short-tempered. He was demanding without being clear about what he wanted. He expected every one of his employees to be as passionate about the business as he was, when for many of them, it was just a job.

Patrick had grown up in a family business, where the children were expected to pitch in from a young age. That was his model of management—parents telling their kids what to do. No wonder he wasn't a very good people manager.

After some tough times in his business, Patrick took a good hard look at himself and realized that all the energy he was putting into being a lousy manager would be much better spent on being a great designer. So he hired a chief operating officer to take over the people management tasks. It was a hard decision. It felt like a failure to him, and it cost him a chunk of money. But it paid off quickly. Turnover plummeted, revenues increased, and Patrick got to focus on what he loved.

In many businesses, the number of people you have reporting to you is a measure of your importance and authority. That leads ambitious people to seek out roles as people leaders, whether or not they like it or have much talent for it. Many specialists, such as scientists, engineers, physicians, lawyers, professors, and other professionals, are astoundingly good at doing the work and astoundingly bad at enabling others to do it.

In summary, one of the key aspects of leading a curated workplace is knowing yourself well enough to seek out leadership roles that fit your abilities and your passions. You'll be able to offer the best you have to your coworkers, and you won't be getting in their way as they try to offer their best.

I want to talk about the concept of curation as it applies to one of the most difficult tasks leaders have to do—firing people. There are a few cruel leaders who enjoy firing people, but most find the task horrifying. As one leader put it, "You know that you are going to have a conversation that will make this one of the worst days of someone's life." Many leaders avoid the task and either keep underperformers in their role much too long or delegate the job of firing people to an underling.

But the right firing, correctly done, is curation in at least two ways. It's curating your team by eliminating a weak performer, which almost certainly will help the other team members perform better and send a clear message about your expectations. And it's also, curiously enough, helping the person you fire to curate his or her own life. The fact is that most people who are poor performers know they're not doing a very good job. They may be hanging on for all sorts of reasons, but deep down they usually know they're not in the right role for them. Being fired, as awful as it is, often serves as the stimulus for them to take a hard look at how they've been curating their work life and move on to something that's better for them. I've never been fired, but I've been downsized twice. And in both cases, that miserable experience was the stimulus for me to move on to my next, much more satisfying role.

Leading for curation includes:

- being a good role model, setting expectations, and protecting people from their unreasonable expectations of themselves;
- creating a culture that reduces fear to foster creativity and innovation;
- evaluating your people thoughtfully so you are assigning rewards in a meaningful manner;
- choosing your battles carefully;
- cultivating your self-awareness so that you seek out leadership roles that fit well with your abilities and passions.

Great leadership for curation also demands that you provide mentorship to your people. Sometimes this is a formal, one-on-one relationship. I would challenge any leader who is mentoring others to deliberately and regularly include curation in your mentorship conversations. For up-and-coming leaders, mastering curation can be a remarkable career accelerator, and failing to do so can cause a serious derailment.

Beyond those one-to-one mentorship relationships, great leaders also think about developing their people's curation skills through broader programs. One of my favorite examples of this comes from an interesting experience I had a few years ago. I had just given a presentation on curating your life when a woman in the audience, Laura, came up to me and told me about a program her boss had recently developed. They called it the Priority Project. Laura's boss, Alejandro, was the head of IT for a large health care company. Leaders of other departments were continually approaching the IT people with requests for services, both big and small. Although the IT department was large, the team members were swamped with requests and exhausted by trying to keep up with everything.

So Alejandro created the Priority Project. Every member of the department was trained in how to sort the requests into three categories—"Mission Critical," "Necessary but not Mission Critical," and "Unnecessary." Alejandro's directive to his people was to focus their energy on the top priority, give moderate attention to the second priority, and deny requests that were in the third priority. Laura and I were both struck by the similarity between my curating model and Alejandro's Priority Project.

The challenge, of course, was that leaders from other departments didn't like it when the IT people classified their requests as "Necessary but not Mission Critical" or "Not Necessary." So I worked with Alejandro and his team to help them develop the communication skills to keep the Priority Project on track. Managing their focus and their energy continued to be a challenge, but the Priority Project gave the IT department a common language and set of tools for increasing their productivity and doing the work that really mattered to the company.

Sometimes a leader can help his or her team members curate their lives through direct instruction and advice. At other times, the leader's influence may be more subtle. The book *Nudge* by Richard Thaler and Cass Sunstein outlines a theory and supporting research on how to affect people's choices by altering the environment in which they make their decisions. For example, suppose you want your employees to contribute part of their paycheck to a retirement plan, which is almost always a really good financial decision. So you give them a form to sign that says, "If you want to set aside x percent of your income for your retirement account, check this box." Chances are that a fairly small percentage will sign up (barely 20 percent in one study). But if you change the default choice—people are automatically enrolled unless they choose to opt out—the percentage of participants jumps to 90 percent.[6] Notice you are not *forcing* anyone to contribute to his or her retirement plan. But by tweaking the environment, you affect people's decision-making. There are numerous other examples of how leaders can do this in the workplace in order to encourage good curation.

Curation can enable you to have a better life yourself. It can also help you create a better work environment for your team. And, equally important, in the next chapter we'll explore how practicing curation can help you make your home a happier, more nourishing place for you and your family.

KEY TAKEAWAYS

- Context has a huge impact on how people act.
- It is the responsibility of leaders to create an environment where people are encouraged and supported to curate their lives.
- Curation is a key element in getting the best performance from your people, both because they are using their energy in a focused and efficient manner and because they are finding meaning and joy in what they are doing.
- Energy curation means helping your people manage their energy wisely. That includes:

    - being a good role model in your own work style;

- setting reasonable expectations for how much time people have to be "on";
- sometimes protecting your people from their unreasonable expectations of themselves.

- Risk curation is about fostering innovation and creativity by reducing fear and enabling your people to differentiate between mission critical work where a cautious approach is wise and other kinds of work where risks can be taken and mistakes can be made.
- Recognition curation is about identifying and rewarding true greatness, using a variety of assessment techniques to get a good understanding of people's performance and potential.
- Employees have a responsibility to help their managers see their greatness by aiming to be High Visibility/Low Maintenance.
- Conflict curation is about focusing your attention on the battles that really matter.
- Self-awareness is essential to ensure that you seek out roles that will encourage and reward your greatness, rather than trying to become someone you are not.
- The horrible experience of firing/being fired can help someone become a better curator of his/her life.

8

MANAGE A CURATED HOME

Back when I was a psychotherapist, I often worked with clients on how to handle their family lives more successfully. We would work on communication skills, conflict management, understanding children's developmental stages, following through on promises—many aspects of how to build healthy family relationships. And very often, my clients would pause, look thoughtful, and say, "You know, I think I could use some of these tactics at work, too."

Flash forward twenty years and now I'm working with my executive coaching clients. We're focusing on how to handle their work lives more successfully. We work on communication skills, conflict management, understanding different kinds of employees, following through on promises—many aspects of building an engaged, productive workplace. And this time around, I hear, "You know, I think I could use some of these tactics at home, too."

Of course, my clients are right. In spite of the fact that we often see work and home as two very different spheres of life, people are people and relationships are relationships. Not every skill transfers perfectly from one realm to another, but many do.

We've already talked about plenty of examples of how curation applies to your personal life. This chapter focuses on you as the leader/manager of your household—how you can help yourself and other family members to be more joyful and productive in the context of your home.

I want to start by specifying that I have never been a believer in the notion that an organization has to have just one boss. I know many people think this to be true—that there has to be a single boss/CEO/head of the household who has the final say. I'm sure there are many fine organizations where this is true. But I also know many high-functioning businesses and families where this is not the case. Successful, equal partnerships are common in both realms.

This makes me think of my friend, Jim, who has had a long and successful marriage and who was in a business partnership with his wife, Daphne, for a while. Jim used to ironically say, "Oh, Daphne and I have it worked out perfectly. She gets to make the small decisions, like what kind of car we should buy and where the kids should go to school. I get to make the big decisions, like who should be the Premier of Ontario and what we should do about the Canadian/American dollar exchange rate." Every organization, whether a family or a business, needs clear decision rules. But there doesn't have to be just one decider.

How can you apply the principles of curation to your home? Once again, it starts with values. When you think about a "success-ful" family, what comes to mind? What really matters to you in your home? An absence of conflict? A lot of laughter? Everyone is beautiful? Your kids all graduate from medical school? What is the legacy you want to pass on? How do you want to be remembered as a spouse, a parent, a grandparent?

Then take a look at how you are spending your energy at home. Are you focusing on the things that really matter, or are you get-ting caught up in unimportant and maybe destructive encounters about unimportant issues?

What does a curated marriage/primary relationship look like? Once again, it's going to be different for different people. For many people, it starts with making choices about how much ener-gy you'll put into meeting the other person's needs and how much into taking care of your own. At the beginning of many relationships, it is so intoxicating to be around the other person that you're willing to do just about anything to be near them and breathe the air they're breathing. But over time, the passion often settles down a bit. Maybe you were fine with going camping back in the early years, but now you dread it. Maybe you used to be OK going to "chick flicks" with your partner but now you feel as if you're going to poke your eye out with a fork if you have to sit through another one. Then the curation gets tougher. How important is it to be with my partner doing something he/she loves? How much will I honor my own needs and preferences?

As I said, there isn't one right answer. But it's a really good idea to be aware of those choices, talk about them, and make them consciously. Some years ago, I realized that I sometimes agreed to an activity I really didn't want to do. (It usually involved water sports, which I don't enjoy and my husband loves.) I would go along on the activity, but I would be unpleasant the whole time. That's a really bad way to curate. When I became aware of the pattern, I made a commitment to myself. If I agreed to go sailing, I would do so wholeheartedly and not be sucky about it. If I couldn't do that, then I would say no. And I would be fine with my husband going sailing with other people when I didn't want to go. I feel better about myself since I made that commitment, and I suspect I'm easier to put up with, too.

Another part of curating your primary relationship is picking your battles. (See, my clients were right—different spheres of life, same skills needed. You might want to revisit Conflict Curation in chapter 7.) In my previous career as a therapist I saw a lot of this problem in couples' counseling. Some couples would fight to the death about who should empty the garbage (in my mind, a relatively unimportant issue that should be easy to negotiate). Others would avoid talking about really crucial disagreements, like whether or not to have a baby. And sometimes I would see couples where one person loved to fight while the other one was conflict-avoidant. All of these patterns come out of our temperament and our life experiences. They can all be changed and moderated to make relationships happier and more productive.

For most couples, this kind of curation is really, really hard. Many of us have poor role models for how to do it. You may have come from a family where people screamed at each other over the most minor disagreements. You may have come from a home where there was physical or emotional abuse. On the other hand, you may have come from a tightly emotionally controlled household where people avoided conflict at all costs.

Different people have different levels of comfort about how battles should be fought and how often. You are very lucky if you and your partner come from families with similar rules about fighting. Even if they aren't great rules, at least you know where the other person is coming from. In any case, I would suggest that none of the patterns in the previous paragraph is optimal. Good conflict curation lies somewhere between constant screaming and stony silence.

Once again, self-awareness is very helpful here. Asia is a good example. In the years when she had young children and her energy was being stretched to the max, she often found herself wildly angry at her husband. She would fume internally about what a jerk he was, how he didn't pull his weight, how he took her for granted, how he left dirty dishes in the sink, and so on. Sometimes she would feel so angry she would fantasize about leaving him.

Then one day she had a surprising realization. These wildly angry feelings usually happened in the early evening when she was preparing dinner. Asia found that if she waited until after she had eaten, the angry feelings usually subsided. She learned that a lot of other women had the same pattern. There was even a word for it, "hangry." So she decided she would always wait until after dinner before she confronted her husband about something. If she was still mad, it was probably an important issue that she needed to deal with. But most of the time, when dinner was finished, she had difficulty even remembering what she had been so furious about.

I counsel my clients that it's usually a good idea to wait before you wade into a conflict, whether at work or at home. So often, our anger is exaggerated by other factors in our environment besides the horribleness of the person we're mad at. Some things are so egregious or urgent that they have to be confronted right away, but most of the time we manage conflict better if we take a pause—a few minutes or a few days, depending on how long your fuse is. If after that time you are still upset, then this issue is important enough to march into battle. Needless to say, once you make the decision to fight, there are a whole bunch of rules of engagement about how to fight effectively. But that's the topic of another book. This one is about curating your battles into: let it go, mention it but don't make a big deal, or confront the problem head-on.

Years ago, I heard a sermon where a rabbi talked about the importance of having a good "forgettery," as opposed to a good memory. If you choose to let something go, you have to let it go. If you can't, then it's important enough to engage in the confrontation.

For many readers, this may be the toughest chapter of all, so be sure to take your break. If your spouse is around, maybe you can go and say something nice to him or her. If you're living with a small child, spending a few minutes with him or her can be a great break. Or you can just go to the kitchen and find something good to munch on.

Marriage is complicated enough. And then we decide to add a whole other level of complexity—children. In my experience, if you have a wonderful relationship, having children will make it worse. If you have a troubled relationship, having children may well end it. I don't mean to sound cynical. For me, having children was a remarkable and wondrous adventure and I wouldn't have missed it for the world. But it ain't easy.

Talk about energy curation! Try having an infant. That kid will take everything you have to offer and then more. Meanwhile, you're still supposed to go to work, maintain your personal hygiene, keep the house under control, and so forth. As I've said before, I'm a list maker and I have always had a list of what I intend to do each day. When my first baby was born, I would get up each morning and make my list—usually about seven or eight simple items. And by the end of the day I would have done maybe one and a half of them. I finally realized the only solution was to stop making the lists for a while.

Eventually most new parents figure out how to get the essential stuff done and they eliminate a bunch of nonessential stuff. But here's another big challenge. As I said earlier, successful marriage is about curating your energy to meet your own needs as well as your partner's. But now you also have to curate your energy between looking after your kids' needs as well as your own and your partner's.

In my experience, many couples make the mistake of overinvesting their energy in their children and underinvesting in their relationship with each other. Don't get me wrong—being a great parent is hugely important to most of us, and that takes a massive amount of energy. But without a strong fundamental bond between the parents, all the other tasks are much harder.

I want to make it clear that I am in no way attacking single parents or saying they can't do a great job with their kids. I am in awe of them. I have never been in their shoes and I don't presume to offer advice on how to curate if you're a single parent, other than—don't try to do this alone. Talk to others who have been there. Find the good books, the support groups (both formal and informal), and the blogs.

If you are in a marriage with kids, don't neglect your relationship. Find a way to look after each other and allot some of your energy to that purpose. My friend Samantha had a good idea. She found a reliable babysitter and put him on a retainer for Saturday nights. In other words, she paid him for several hours of babysitting every weekend whether or not she needed him, and he held his Saturday nights for her family. The result was that she and her husband could go out spontaneously on Saturday nights. Sometimes they went off to a wonderful play or concert. Other times they just went around the corner for a beer and nachos. They knew they would have their Saturday nights to bring their energy to each other, and that helped all through the week when things got crazy.

If you think curation is tough when the kids are little, it's a whole other game when they're adolescents. Research on marital satisfaction generally shows that people are happiest in their marriages before they have children and after the kids leave home.[1] For many couples the most difficult time is when they have teenagers at home. Parenting teenagers sucks up a huge amount of energy. There is often a lot of conflict in the home. The teenagers' developmental issues often trigger memories of the parents' own adolescent challenges. How often have you seen a parent arguing with a teenager and wondered which person is the adolescent?

Teenagers take up so much emotional space that the easiest path is to pretty much ignore your spouse. In fact, you and your partner may disagree on how to handle the kids, which increases the distance between you. But once again, if you would like your relationship to survive the next decade, then you'd better adjust your curation to ensure that you and your partner are getting some high-quality time together. Easy to say, hard to do—but if having a great relationship is important to you, then you have to curate accordingly.

Another difficult aspect of curating when you have teenagers is helping your teen begin to curate his or her own life. A lot of young people today are suffering from massive overcommitment. In many families, the expectations for teenagers are brutal. They have to make top grades, be outstanding athletes, develop their musical abilities, engage in community service—the list goes on and on. Often this is because parents fear that unless their children are superstars in everything, they won't succeed in life. They won't get into the right schools, and then they won't get good jobs, and then they won't be able to find good partners, and then they'll just be bums.

This is absurd. And it's terrible for the teenagers. Kids under this kind of pressure are at risk for medical problems, alcoholism, drug abuse, and even suicide. Of course, as a parent you want your children to succeed and excel. But learning how to curate is one of the essential life skills they need in order to sustain themselves and be productive and happy over the long term. It's your job to teach them how to do that. So talk with them about their values and their dreams. Help them to get clear on what really matters to them, where they can be just good enough, and what activities they should just forget about for now. Often it's a good idea to let them quit stuff they hate, even if that means giving up part of your dreams for them.

Robert was born into a family of avid musicians. To the delight of his parents, he showed extraordinary musical talent from a very young age. They encouraged his musical development, hiring the best teachers for him and focusing on his practice time at home. By his early teens he was performing as a soloist with a professional orchestra and after high school he graduated from a very prestigious conservatory. His parents were deeply involved in supporting his professional career.

And then he stopped playing. He fell in love with a woman who wasn't particularly interested in music and didn't want him to have a professional musical career. That gave him the excuse he needed to step away from music, which had ceased to be a source of joy for him. When the couple married, Robert's parents were deeply disappointed because he was giving up his musical career, which meant so much to them. Eventually he went back to playing for fun, but he never performed professionally again. He told me, "I believed that my parents loved me only because of my playing."

My guess is that he was wrong about that—that they loved him for himself, as most parents love their children. But something had gone very wrong in their relationship for him to feel that way. Chances are his parents were overinvested in Robert's musical success, which made it almost impossible for him to make his own curation choices as he grew up. Ultimately, he was able to make the right choice for himself, but only with a great deal of pain.

Let's not do that to our kids, especially as they become young adults. Instead let's teach them how to listen to their own passions and find their own greatness.

Then there's the Empty Nest phase. When my sons were all still at home, I had a friend, Sheila, whose youngest son was the age of my oldest son. She was sort of a mentor to me. When I thought about my sons leaving home, I had a feeling of real sadness and dread. So I turned to Sheila for reassurance. I said to her, "I suppose that when the time comes I'll be ready for them to leave." To my dismay, Sheila burst into tears.

Not all parents find it hard when their children leave home, but I sure did. Even though each of my sons was a real handful in the last year of high school, when each one left home I was really sad and lonely for several months. I felt like an idiot, because of course I wanted them to grow up and be independent—but I really missed them. After a while it got better. To this day, I am always glad when they come home, but I'm no longer devastated when they leave.

In fact, truth be told, the Empty Nest phase has been great for me. I have been able to take the energy I was pouring into my kids and use it to build a new phase of my career. My husband and I have more freedom to enjoy our time together. My home feels well-curated, which is a wonderful feeling.

Before I end this chapter, I want to talk about curation in the context of extended family relationships. Most of us have close family connections that go beyond our nuclear family. Those relationships can be a great source of energy and joy—but they also *take* energy (duh—who knew?). As you're curating your life, where does your mother-in-law fit in? Your brother with medical issues? Your grandchildren?

When Ellen's children were still young, she realized that her aging parents needed more help. They lived about an hour away from Ellen, and she and her husband were often being called on to help with medical issues and other crises. So they decided to invite Ellen's parents to move in with them. They sold both houses and bought a bigger house that could encompass everyone.

It was a loving and thoughtful choice, but it was very difficult. All the routines that Ellen and her family were used to were turned upside down. Ellen found herself emotionally and physically overwhelmed by trying to manage the challenges of her new-ly expanded household.

As we were talking about her dismay, we decided to do the math. When Ellen was living with her husband and two kids, there were six relationships in the household:

- Ellen and her husband
- Ellen and Kid 1
- Ellen and Kid 2
- Husband and Kid 1
- Husband and Kid 2
- Kid 1 and Kid 2

What happened to the number of relationships in the household when Grandma and Grandpa moved in? Two more relationships? Try nine more! In addition to the six above, they now had:

- Ellen and Grandma
- Ellen and Grandpa
- Husband and Grandma
- Husband and Grandpa
- Kid 1 and Grandma
- Kid 1 and Grandpa
- Kid 2 and Grandma
- Kid 2 and Grandpa
- Grandma and Grandpa

No wonder Ellen was overwhelmed! Living with her aging parents never got easy, but just realizing how much her life had increased in complexity helped Ellen to cut herself some slack and find some energy to look after her own needs once in a while.

There are many other examples of how you can apply the prin-ciples of curation to your home life. Once again, it's about decid-ing what's important and putting your energy there. It's about saying no to the things that just don't matter that much, being so-so on a whole bunch of things, and giving your absolute best to where you choose to be great. I know that many people's homes are fraught with conflict, anger, disappointment, frustration—the list goes on and on. How much harder it is to go out in the world and be great if your home life is sucking up most of your energy.

In the best scenario, your home becomes a place that *gives* you energy rather than draining you. It is a safe haven from the demands and challenges of the big, bad world. Of course, that cannot possibly be true all the time. But in the immortal words of Captain Picard, at least some of the time you can "make it so."

KEY TAKEAWAYS

- Figure out what is a successful family in your set of values, and then assess whether you are allotting your energy to match those priorities.
- Relationship curation is about balancing your needs with your partner's, picking your battles appropriately, and making your relationship a priority.
- Kid curation is about giving huge amounts of energy to your children, helping your teenagers curate their own lives in a healthy manner, and keeping yourself and your relationship going through all those demands.
- Relationships with your extended family members, especially living in the same house, add another level of complexity to family curation.
- The goal is to make your home a safe haven where you can draw energy to tackle the other challenges of your life.

9

RE-CURATE

When I was a child, one of my favorite things in the whole, wide world was going to the Museum of Science and Industry in Chicago. I can still remember the exhibits so vividly—the math exhibit with ping pong balls showing how probability works, Yesterday's Main Street with a theater showing silent movies, the farm with tractors and models of animals, the Fairy Castle, the chicks hatching out of eggs, the giant beating heart, the enormous train layout, the Coal Mine. The whole thing was just spectacularly wonderful.

I recently went back to the Museum with my granddaughter. To my dismay, some of the exhibits I loved are gone, and others have been dramatically changed. I was really quite peeved, because I wanted to show her the museum I remembered.

But you know what? The world of 2020 is not the world of 1962. Some of the exhibits that were so special to me then would seem laughably out-of-date and boring now. The curators at the Museum of Science and Industry had the good sense to realize that for the museum to remain special and relevant, they had to re-curate. Not everything had to go—but many changes had to be made as the years went by.

Guess what—the same is true of life curation. You're going to have to re-curate from time to time. As you move through your life, there will be times when you'll take down some of the "paintings" and hang other ones, or at least move them around. We change, the world around us changes, and so our curation has to change.

There was a time when psychologists theorized that our cognitive and emotional development ended when we reached adulthood. Theorists like Sigmund Freud[1] and Jean Piaget[2] proposed various frameworks for the stages of childhood development. Don't get me wrong—I think Freud and Piaget and many of the other early psychologists were geniuses. Much of their work has stood the test of time very well.

But while these early thinkers blazed the way, their theories were incomplete. The notion that one is psychologically finished at around age twenty doesn't fit the reality of our lives. One of the first psychologists to extend developmental theory into adulthood was Erik Erikson. Erikson proposed the model that is illustrated in figure 9.1.

As you can see, there are five stages of child development, but they are followed by three stages of adult development with different issues to be resolved at each stage.[3] Other theorists of adult development followed, including Daniel Levinson,[4] Roger Gould,[5] Bernice Neugarten,[6] and many others. Gail Sheehy published her book *Passages* in 1976, in which she popularized the work of many experts in the field.[7]

As both an observer of and a participant in the challenges of adult development, I am convinced that psychological development is a lifelong process. Some experts in adult development have proposed that adults do not experience just one "mid-life crisis."[8] Instead we experience a series of developmental crises. At each stage of our life, we make choices that satisfy some aspects of ourselves at the expense of other parts. For example, when you choose to get married, you satisfy your hunger for intimacy, security, stability, family identity, and so on. But you no longer get to fulfill your desire for sexual adventures with a variety of people, for isolation, or for the freedom to please yourself without regard for your partner's needs.

Figure 9.1. Erikson's stages of psychosocial development. *Mary Clare Butler*

The same process unfolds in your work life. My client Greg is a good example. Greg was a brilliant student at an elite university, and upon graduation he landed a highly desirable job in finance. The job was incredibly demanding and required constant travel. It was exhausting, and it also didn't give Greg much of a sense that he was doing good in the world. But that didn't matter a lot to him. The job paid a bucket-load of money and it satisfied his competitive spirit.

But after a while, those parts of yourself you have neglected start to give you trouble and you have to re-evaluate your choices and priorities. Sometimes these "crises" are fairly small, and you can redesign your life with a few minor tweaks. At other times the crisis is a major upheaval and you will make big changes in how you organize your life.

You may have noticed the verbs I used in the previous paragraph—reevaluate, redesign, make big changes in how you organize your life. Another way of saying all of those things is "recurate."

When Greg reached his early thirties, he began to resent his job. He had made a lot of money, but he had no social life and his work felt pointless. He plugged away for a while, but he came to see me when he realized he really had to make a change. Together we explored his options and he decided to leave his job and create a start-up to work on one of his ideas. At a tech incubator he met a fiery, intelligent young woman who became his wife. He now has two children and he continues to work hard. But he is in control of his schedule and curates his life to use much of his energy for his family.

Changing your priorities doesn't mean you were doing the wrong things before. Your curation may have been beautifully designed for that phase of your life. But no curation is going to last forever, any more than a museum exhibit should stay the same for all eternity.

Anita was a sad example of a failure to re-curate. She was a very successful financial analyst who made a lot of money for herself and her clients. She enjoyed the intellectual challenge of her work, the competition, and the triumphant feeling of creating prosperity for her own family and for others. In mid-career, she was invited to join a very prestigious wealth management firm. After a couple of years, she realized that some of the firm's practices were unethical. Anita was fearful that if she became a whistle-blower, she would lose her stature and wealth, so she kept silent. But she began investing less and less energy in her work and her results started to suffer. Anita felt paralyzed in her situation and began to drink heavily. Eventually she was fired from her job, retired early, and whiled away her days doing not much of anything.

As I said, sometimes you have to re-curate because your needs and priorities have changed. Another time re-curation is essential is when you get a big job promotion. Marshall Goldsmith wrote a classic book about leadership, *What Got You Here Won't Get You*

There.[9] The book outlines a dilemma that many leaders face when they get promoted. They know they got their promotion because they did really good work in their previous role. So naturally their instinct is to keep doing that work as well as they can. Except now that they've been promoted, that's not their job anymore. In fact, if they keep doing their old job, two bad things will happen. First, they won't be learning to excel at the responsibilities that came with their new role. Second, they will be driving their team crazy because they'll be micromanaging the work and not giving their team members room to learn and grow.

In order to succeed at their new role, they have to re-curate. They have to let go of activities that are not critically important to their new job, even if they love doing them. And they have to figure out where their greatness will now lie.

Two of my clients come to mind. Jeremy was a vice president at a financial services firm. He was a highly successful business developer and client account manager who loved being out on the road meeting with current and potential clients. When he was promoted to senior vice president, he continued to spend at least half his time traveling. Meanwhile, his team was floundering without his presence and leadership. I helped him to recognize that he needed to re-curate and focus more of his energy on his internal responsibilities. He continued to spend some time traveling to the most lucrative clients, but he spent more time developing the talents of his team members so they became highly effective business developers and client managers as well.

Austin was a highly talented executive vice president who excelled at designing and leading superb operations. Others knew they could rely on him to take a new idea and make it into a reality. But when he was designated as the successor to the CEO, he realized he had to turn more of his attention to strategic issues. His company was in an industry that was changing very rapidly, and the next CEO would need to provide a clear vision of how to navigate both the predictable and the unseen challenges that lay ahead. Austin and I worked together to adjust his schedule, so he set aside designated time for strategic thinking and planning.

When he was promoted to CEO, he was ready to lead the company to new levels of success.

When do you have to re-curate? Whenever what is most important to you changes. Common transition times include:

- leaving school and entering the workforce
- entering a committed relationship
- the birth of each child (especially the first one!)
- changing jobs
- a big promotion
- moving to a new community
- leaving a committed relationship
- health crises
- death of a parent, a child, a spouse, or another loved one
- retirement

I was surprised to find that becoming a grandmother turned out to be a big re-curation challenge for me. I was very much looking forward to grandchildren, but I was not prepared for the powerful emotional impact of meeting my children's children. I felt the same fierce protectiveness toward my grandchildren that I had felt toward my own children. And within a few months I realized that my priorities had undergone a tectonic shift. Being great at grandparenting was hugely important to me.

Luckily for me, my grandchildren lived nearby and I had the opportunity to see them frequently. But even though they were a source of enormous joy, the fact was that they took a *lot* of energy. There's a good reason why people typically become parents in their twenties and thirties rather than in their sixties!

If I was going to be great at grandparenting, I had to answer the key question of re-curation: What am I going to do less of? Let's face it. Very few people who hold down demanding jobs are sitting around staring into space and wondering what to do with themselves. We're *busy*! In fact, we're often more than busy, we're crazed. So if I'm going to add something to my life, especially something that's as big a deal as grandparenting, what am I going to do less of?

If you can't think of something you're willing to do less of, then you can't add the new activity to your life. It's that simple. Remember your four-burner stove—how many pots can you cook at one time? What happens if you want to cook more pots than you have burners? If you can't take one of the pots off, then you can't put one on.

So, just as I did when I became a mother, I had to let go of some of the things I was doing, including some that were meaningful and fun. I don't take classes as much as I used to. I spend less time on business development for my company. My social life is somewhat curtailed. But as a result, I can spend Wednesday evenings and all day on Fridays with my beloved grandchildren. Is it worth it? You bet.

Ready to take a break? Maybe you'd like to listen to some music. Put on one of your favorite songs or pieces and put your whole attention on listening to it. Decide if you want to be energized or soothed and make your choice accordingly.

Sometimes the world around you changes and you have to respond. And there are many other times when you can feel it in your psyche—something is out of whack, and it's time to make a change, to re-curate.

Sam was an investment analyst by training. He liked his work and was good at it. His wife, Lisa, was a brilliant, ambitious woman who founded and built a very successful small advertising agency. Tragically, she developed a very aggressive cancer in her late thirties and died within a few months. Sam was heartbroken, and at the same time he felt a commitment to preserve the company she had worked so hard to build. For the next three years, he did his best to keep the company going, and thanks to a talented staff, the company prospered. But Sam came to see me when he recognized that as a leader he had two big problems. First, he wasn't a skilled advertising executive. He couldn't provide the creative or techni-

cal leadership that the team needed. Second, and more importantly, advertising wasn't his passion. He didn't hate it, but he didn't
love it either.

It was time for Sam to re-curate. He had chosen greatness—
greatness as a husband who wanted to preserve his beloved wife's
legacy. But he recognized that it was time for him to step back into
his own life trajectory and return to the investment world. I
helped Sam to identify a successor for his company's leadership
and to manage the transition process. Thanks to Sam's caring ste-
wardship and his intelligent decision to step back when the time
was right, the company continued to prosper. And Sam was able to
return to the work where his greatness lay.

This kind of re-curation can be very difficult for business leaders, especially founders. Starting and growing a company is a very
personal endeavor, and often the leader's identity is bound up in
his/her role with the company. Recognizing when it is time to step
away, both for the company's sake and for the leader's sake, can be
very tough.

Successfully navigating this kind of re-curation depends in part
on understanding what kind of leader you are. Some of us are
start-up guys. Some of us love turn-arounds. Some people are
great at "maintain and grow." When the fit isn't right between
what the leader loves to do and is good at and what the company
needs, it's time to re-curate.

One of my clients, Larry, was a very intelligent, charismatic
leader. Together with some friends he started a small tech company that grew steadily. As CEO, Larry focused on two goals: first,
attracting top talent by making the company a great place to work,
and second, providing impeccable client service. The company
thrived. By the time the workforce reached one hundred people,
Larry was bored. He was still doing a good job, but the kinds of
problems he was now tackling were not especially interesting to
him. So he brought in a seasoned second-in-command and gradually increased the new leader's scope of responsibilities. By the
time Larry was ready to walk away, his second-in-command was

prepared to take over the reins. Larry went on to start another company, and his first company continued to grow and prosper.

However, as I said, for many leaders it is not so easy to step away from a role that has been your passion and your identity for many years. It is hard to believe that anyone else could possibly fill your shoes. And these leaders often have been so focused on their work that they have no idea what they're going to do with themselves afterward.

Years ago, I was invited to speak about succession planning to a group of senior leaders of Jewish nonprofit organizations, mostly older men who had been in their roles for many years. After speaking with them about best practices in succession planning, I told them I was going to share with them a case study of one of the most difficult succession planning challenges in the history of the world—the passage of leadership from Moses to Joshua.

Of course, there are many aspects of that story that are not directly relevant to most modern leadership transitions, including the fact that God chose the successor. But if you read through the story in the Bible, you'll find startlingly modern ideas about how to successfully manage a leadership transition. First—qualifications. Joshua is chosen as the successor because he is "inspired," which is a critically important qualification for a leader then and now (Numbers 27:18). Moses is instructed to "invest him with your authority" in a public ceremony (Numbers 27:19–20). That sets Joshua up for success in the eyes of the people. Moses gives Joshua clear direction and a mission to fulfill, and encourages him to be confident and courageous (Deuteronomy 31:7–8). He includes Joshua in a very important meeting (Deuteronomy 31:14). The community takes time to honor and let go of the previous leader, Moses, before transferring their loyalty to the new leader, Joshua (Deuteronomy 34:8–9). And then the new leader, Joshua, steps right into action, carrying on the traditions and teachings of the previous leader, Moses (Joshua 1:1–18).

This story is fascinating to me because, as I said, it seems so up-to-date in how to handle a leadership transition. But it's also thought-provoking on an emotional level. It was very difficult for

Moses to let go of his leadership role. According to Jewish legend, he was grief-stricken that he could not complete his task and lead the People of Israel into the Promised Land. But nonetheless, he followed good succession planning practices, he set Joshua up for success, and then he stepped away.

When I gave this talk to the organizational leaders, I ended with this: "Our great teacher, Moses, spent his entire life teaching us how to live. And even in his death he teaches us. Because, ultimately, we will all leave our work unfinished. Nobody gets to see the story through to the end. But we can ensure that the story will continue, even without us, by passing the mantle of leadership to the next person and stepping gracefully out of the scene."

I'll tell you, there were plenty of tears in the audience. Letting go of a treasured role is one of the most difficult re-curating challenges. The good news is that we have some excellent role models for how to navigate this task successfully.

Sometimes the transitions of re-curation are relatively easy, but often they're difficult. Change is always challenging—giving up parts of your life that have been important to you in order to adapt to a new phase. Chaim Potok said, "All beginnings are hard,"[10] but I would add, "So are all transitions."

My good friends, Gary and Vicki Pines, are at an age when many people start thinking about retirement. They are youthful and vigorous, they enjoy their work, and they don't plan to retire any time soon. But once a year they sit down together for what they call their "re-balancing" conversation. They talk about how they are using their time, what they are enjoying, what they would like to do more or less of, their financial priorities, and so on. They make a plan together for the coming year. They call it re-balancing. I would call it re-curating—and it's a great idea for couples who want to stay connected and vibrant.

In my mind, *the most important task of adult development is to figure out what is important and put your energy into that.* It sounds simple—but it takes a lifetime of experimentation, openness, and determination to get it right.

KEY TAKEAWAYS

- No curation lasts forever.
- Psychological development continues in adulthood.
- Re-curation is necessary when you change or when your circumstances change.
- Before you take on new goals and responsibilities, you have to ask yourself, "What will I do less of?"
- Letting go of a leadership role and handing it over to your successor is one of the hardest re-curation challenges.
- The most important task of adult development is to figure out what is important and put your energy into that.

10

BUST LOOSE—DISCIPLINE AND LIBERATION

There is a paradox at the core of curating your life. This is a book about discipline—about making conscious choices in your life and then following through on those decisions. It is about living each day with an awareness of what is important and consistently focusing your energy on those goals. That's hard work.

And at the same time, this is a book about liberation—about freeing yourself to live joyfully and with meaning. It is about letting go of the multitude of distractions that are preventing you from finding and living your greatness.

Discipline and freedom—they are inextricably bound together. *You cannot be truly free without discipline.* You will be enslaved by your impulses, by instant gratification, by mindlessness.

You also cannot be truly disciplined without freedom. Even the strictest regimen must allow for some rule-breaking. Across the world, almost all cultures have some kind of ritualized rule-breaking. Americans have Halloween, when we dress up in ridiculous costumes, eat way too much candy, and encourage our children to go door-to-door begging from and threatening our neighbors with "Trick or Treat." We have New Year's Eve, when we drink too much, wear silly hats, blow noisemakers, and generally misbehave.

Brits have Guy Fawkes Day, Catholics have Mardi Gras, Jews have Purim.

We all need to bust loose sometimes. Just yesterday I had set aside three hours to work on this book. I was feeling low energy, so I thought, "I'll take a break and just watch twenty minutes of a movie on TV." Three hours later I was still in front of the TV set and my writing time was shot.

One of my clients, Julia, was a very organized, disciplined person. She was punctual. She was unfailingly polite to people. She exercised regularly. But she figured out there were three areas of her life where discipline was a challenge for her: how she ate, how she spent money, and how she used her time. And here's the kicker. She learned she couldn't master all three of those challenges at the same time. If she was eating wisely and watching her budget, she was going to be wasting time. If she was careful about her money and keeping a strict schedule, she'd be eating too much. And if she was eating well and keeping her time commitments, her credit card balance was going to shoot up. She could choose which two to focus on at any time, but it was unrealistic to expect herself to manage all three challenges at once.

Remember the concept of "ego depletion" from chapter 6? None of us can be disciplined in everything all the time. But once again, you have choices. Where and when am I going to cut loose? How can I break the rules without completely derailing my life? How can I give myself permission to be "bad" once in a while without beating myself up about it? And how do I get back on track afterward?

First, it's important to listen to yourself and your needs. If you're tired, the best thing to do is rest. If you're lonely, connect with someone. If you're bored, take a break and do something different. If you're antsy, get up and move around.

Don't pretend you're not feeling what you're feeling. If you avoid or deny your feelings, they'll just gain more power over you. Listen to yourself—and then make choices.

And don't tell yourself you shouldn't feel what you're feeling. Someone once told me, "Feelings don't have brains." I don't entirely agree with that statement, because we know that how you think about something affects how you feel about it. [1]

But at the same time, feelings are often not rational. Saying to yourself that you shouldn't feel what you're feeling or giving yourself a guilt trip for your feelings doesn't enable you to manage your feelings effectively. Beating yourself up for what you are feeling just makes you feel *worse*, and then you are more likely to do something really stupid and self-defeating.

Gina used to do that with anger. She was a psychotherapist and had worked with hundreds of clients who had anger issues. She was endlessly empathic with their feelings of rage or frustration, giving them permission to express what they were feeling in a safe and nonjudgmental space. As far as she was concerned, everyone had a right to their anger and it was her job to help them work through it.

Everyone had a right to anger—except Gina. She told herself she was never supposed to be angry. If she was angry, she was being immature. She had such a good and wonderful life, so she had no right at all to be disappointed or irritable and frustrated. Her anger was always because she was somehow failing to be the person she should be. Anger was just fine for everyone else, but not for Gina.

There were two reasons why that really didn't work. First, suppressing her anger meant that the people around her didn't know she was upset, so they kept on doing the things that were bugging her. Second, on rare occasions all that bottled-up anger would erupt in a very ferocious way. Gina was never abusive to people, but she sure could let fly. People who witnessed those scenes didn't forget them quickly. In those moments, she was impulsive, unkind, and she sometimes did damage to her relationships.

It took Gina years of growing up and some excellent therapy to get to the place where she allowed herself to be mildly or moderately angry on a regular basis. She still doesn't like being in angry mode, and she tries to move through it as quickly as she can, but she no longer ignores and denies her own anger.

So do yourself a favor and listen to your feelings. Use them as data to make good choices about when to follow the rules and when to cut yourself some slack.

I am a great fan of the "Gray Zone." Let me explain. The White Zone is where I want to live most of the time. The White Zone is living with discipline and maturity and compassion and good ethics, being the kind of human being I want to be and the kind of person I would like others to be. The Black Zone is a place I never want to visit. It is where I would do things that are really wrong— cheat on my husband, steal from my employer, ruin a person's reputation, drive drunk, and so on.

In between is the Gray Zone. In the Gray Zone I'm not living my exemplary life, but I'm not being *really bad* either. I'm being a little bit bad. I'm eating six chocolates at once. I'm buying a pretty new necklace when I already have 2,472 necklaces. I'm drinking a full-size martini when I know it will make me silly. I'm watching a movie on TV when I'm supposed to be writing my book.

Gray Zone behaviors are not really harmful, just a little unwise. I think we all need to visit the Gray Zone sometimes. In fact, I like "dancing in the Gray Zone." That's when I'm not only breaking the rules a little bit. I'm thoroughly enjoying it and maybe even calling attention to myself.

In order to safely spend some time in the Gray Zone, you have to be really clear about boundaries. You have to know the difference between the Gray Zone and the White Zone. Being clear about this boundary enables you to cut loose without beating yourself up excessively.

One of the boundaries in my life is that I keep kosher. That means I don't eat pork or shellfish, as well as a host of other rules and restrictions. Once in a long while, if I want to be *really bad*, I sneak out and eat *treif*—food that is not kosher. It's great—all I have to do is eat a piece of bacon and my need for naughtiness can be satisfied. There's something to be said for boundaries.

Even more important, you have to know the difference between the Gray Zone and the Black Zone. Here's an example:

Jerry was sent to me for coaching because he was in big trouble at work. A well-respected professional, he was usually a fairly reserved person. But at company parties he drank too much and then said really vulgar things to women. After several of these events, one of the women complained to Human Resources and Jerry was put on notice—fix this problem or you're out of a job.

For most people, having a drink or two at a company party is Gray Zone behavior. It increases the risk that we may say or do something silly, but most of us can enjoy ourselves with a little alcohol in our system. Not Jerry. One drink and he was in the Black Zone. So we discussed his options. In order to keep himself and others safe, he could go to company parties and not drink any alcohol. Or he could stay away from the parties altogether. He needed to figure out where the boundary was for him.

In fact, Jerry decided to quit drinking entirely for a while, and then to never drink at a company event again. He has maintained this boundary and continues to be a respected leader at his company.

Here's another example. Kim, a married woman with two young children, was away from home at a professional conference. One of her colleagues, Jordan, was also at the conference and they decided to organize a dinner outing with a number of their friends. But one by one the others backed out, so it was just Kim and Jordan going to the dinner. They went off to a very good restaurant, where they enjoyed cocktails, an excellent meal, and some engaging conversation.

When they got back to their hotel, Jordan walked Kim to her room. And in that moment, after enjoying a really delightful evening together, Kim realized she was feeling sexually attracted to Jordan. The two of them stood at her door for a moment, and then Jordan said, "You know, we could go into your room and have a really fun time together. And we'd both feel awful about it afterward." He gave her a gentle hug and walked away. That's what I mean about understanding the difference between the Gray Zone and the Black Zone.

Besides clarity about boundaries, another essential skill for playing in the Gray Zone is knowing how to find your way back to the White Zone. A good example comes from WW (formerly Weight Watchers). Members of WW go to weekly meetings where they learn tips to help them eat in a healthy manner. WW meetings sometimes focus on seasonal challenges to wise eating, and one of the biggies is Thanksgiving. One of the intelligent sayings at WW is, "It doesn't matter what you eat on Thanksgiving. It matters what you eat on the *day after* Thanksgiving." You're probably going to eat too much on Thanksgiving, so enjoy it, but then get back on track the next day. In other words, it doesn't matter so much what you do in the Gray Zone. It matters that you swiftly get yourself back into the White Zone.

One way to maintain the discipline of curating your life without feeling as if you're in a straitjacket is to give yourself permission to cut loose every once in a while.

So, speaking of cutting loose, how about taking your break? Only this time, maybe you don't want to be so disciplined about it. Maybe you want to eat a cookie instead of a piece of fruit. Maybe you want to turn on some silly rerun on television and watch it a little longer than you really should. Maybe this break could be in the Gray Zone?

Here's another way of thinking about the difference between the Gray Zone and the Black Zone. I call it "Golden's Ten-Year Rule." Basically, if you're not going to remember something ten years from now, then it's generally not worth worrying about. The rule helps you to make choices about how to cut loose. It also helps you not to stress out over relatively minor problems. The rule is very useful in both your personal life and your work life. You can get so deadly serious about what you're doing, everything seems like a life-and-death issue. So step back, take a breath, and ask yourself, "Am I going to remember this ten years from now?" If not, don't sweat it. (Please note, I am not talking about memory loss due to alcoholic blackouts or drug use. As far as I'm concerned, that's Black Zone behavior.)

Whether you choose to stay in the White Zone or visit the Gray Zone, the key is to be *present*. Let go of guilt and enjoy what you're doing. Tell yourself, "This is the most valuable thing for me to do right now." (Of course, if you're in the Black Zone, you *should* be feeling guilty. Get yourself out of there fast and mop up the mess you've made!)

So that's it. You have my best thoughts on how to curate your life. It's your life—the only one you get as far as we know. So take charge and be your own curator.

I once thought about what my days would be like if I succeeded in curating my life. Here's what I came up with for me. Every day I would:

- wake up refreshed
- take a quiet moment to look forward to the day
- eat good meals
- work hard
- get stuff done that matters
- enjoy my co-workers
- get some exercise
- have some good time with family/friends
- learn something new
- appreciate my good fortune
- have some fun
- go to bed at a reasonable hour and sleep well

That's my perfect day. It might not be yours. Create your own vision, both as a way of measuring how well you're doing and as an inspiration to stay on track with your curation.

Discipline and liberation—they go together. My heartfelt wish for you is that you curate your life so you reach your greatness, find meaning, and experience deep and abiding joy.

KEY TAKEAWAYS

- Discipline and freedom are bound together. You cannot be truly free without discipline. You will be enslaved by your impulses, by instant gratification, by mindlessness. You also cannot be truly disciplined without freedom.
- No one can be disciplined in everything all the time. But once again, you have choices. Ask yourself:

  - Where and when am I going to cut loose?
  - How can I break the rules without completely derailing my life?
  - How can I give myself permission to be "bad" once in a while without beating myself up about it?
  - How do I get back on track afterward?

- Don't pretend you're not feeling what you're feeling. And don't tell yourself you shouldn't feel what you're feeling.
- Live in the White Zone. Spend a little time in the Gray Zone, being a little bit bad. Stay out of the Black Zone.
- Know the boundaries.
- Live your vision.

NOTES

1. DON'T BALANCE, CURATE

1. Jerry Suls, René Martin, and Ladd Wheeler, "Social Comparison: Why, with Whom, and with What Effect?" *Current Directions in Psychological Science* 11, no. 5 (October 2002): 159–63.

2. James Campbell Quick and Lois E. Tetrick (eds.), *Handbook of Occupational Health Psychology*, 2nd edition (Washington, DC: American Psychological Association, 2011).

3. Kara A. Arnold et al., "Transformational Leadership and Psychological Well-Being: The Mediating Role of Meaningful Work," *Journal of Occupational Health Psychology* 12, no. 3 (2007): 193–203.

4. Jim Loehr and Tony Schwartz, *The Power of Full Engagement* (New York: The Free Press, 2003).

5. Ronald J. Burke, "Working to Live or Living to Work: Should Individuals and Organizations Care?" *Journal of Business Ethics* 84, Supplement 2 (2009): 167–72.

2. DECIDE WHAT'S IMPORTANT

1. Eliot R. Smith and Jamie DeCoster, "Dual-Process Models in Social and Cognitive Psychology: Conceptual Integration and Links to

Underlying Memory Systems," *Personality and Social Review* 4, no. 2 (2000): 108–31.

2. Jim Loehr and Tony Schwartz, *The Power of Full Engagement* (New York: The Free Press, 2003), 218–19.

3. Nancy L. Sin and Sonja Lyubomirsky, "Enhancing Well-Being and Alleviating Depressive Symptoms with Positive Psychology Interventions: A Practice-Friendly Meta-Analysis," *Journal of Clinical Psychology: In Session* 65, no. 5 (2009): 467–87.

3. SAY NO

1. Janet T. Spence and Ann S. Robbins, "Workaholism: Definition, Measurement, and Preliminary Results," *Journal of Personality Assessment* 58, no. 1 (1992): 160–78.

2. Manuel J. Smith, *When I Say No, I Feel Guilty* (New York: Bantam Books, 1975).

4. EMBRACE MEDIOCRITY

1. Julian H. Childs and Joachim Stoeber, "Do You Want Me to Be Perfect? Two Longitudinal Studies on Socially Prescribed Perfectionism, Stress and Burnout in the Workplace," *Work and Stress* 26, no. 4 (2012): 347–64.

2. Catherine H. Tinsley and Robin J. Ely, "What Most People Get Wrong about Men and Women: Research Shows the Sexes Aren't So Different," *Harvard Business Review* 96, no. 3 (May–June 2018): 114–21.

3. Michael E. Porter and Nitin Nohria, "How CEOs Manage Time," *Harvard Business Review* 96, no. 4 (July–August 2018): 42–51.

5. CHOOSE GREATNESS

1. Abraham H. Maslow, "A Theory of Human Motivation," *Psychological Review* 50, no. 4 (1943): 370–96.

2. Robin M. Kowalski and Annie McCord, "If I Knew Then What I Know Now: Advice to My Younger Self," *The Journal of Social Psychology* (2019): 1–20.

3. Keith Ferrazzi with Tal Raz, *Never Eat Alone and Other Secrets to Success, One Relationship at a Time* (New York: Doubleday, 2005).

6. LIVE YOUR GREATNESS

1. Malcolm Gladwell, *Outliers: The Story of Success* (New York: Little Brown and Company, 2008).

2. Laura Warner and Paul Monahan, "Using Audience Commitment to Increase Behavior Changes in Sustainable Landscaping," IFAS Publication Number #WC154 (Gainesville: University of Florida Institute of Food and Agricultural Science). Retrieved from: http://edis.ifas.ufl.edu/wc154.

3. Monique Boekaerts, Moshe Zeiden, and Paul R. Pintrich, *Handbook of Self-Regulation* (San Diego: Academic Press, 2000), 25.

4. Gary P. Latham and Gerard Seijts, "Learning Goals or Performance Goals: Is It the Journey or the Destination?" *Ivey Business Journal* (May/June 2006). Retrieved from https://iveybusinessjournal.com/publication/learning-goals-or-performance-goals-is-it-the-journey-or-the-destination/.

5. Barbara L. Fredrickson, "Positive Emotions Broaden and Build," *Advances in Experimental Social Psychology* 47 (2013), 1–53.

7. CURATE YOUR WORKPLACE

1. Malcolm Gladwell, *Outliers: The Story of Success* (New York: Little Brown and Company, 2008).

2. Arianna Huffington, *The Sleep Revolution: Transforming Your Life, One Night at a Time* (New York: Harmony Books, 2016).

3. Kelly Leonard and Tom Yorton, *Yes, And* (New York: Harper Business, 2015).

4. Joseph Heller, *Something Happened* (New York: Ballantine Books, 1974), 9–13.

5. Andrea S. Kramer and Alton B. Harris, *Breaking Through Bias* (Brookline, MA: Bibliomotion, 2016).

6. Richard H. Thaler and Cass R. Sunstein, *Nudge: Improving Decisions about Health, Wealth, and Happiness* (New York: Penguin Books, 2008), 111.

8. MANAGE A CURATED HOME

1. Brian D. Doss et al., "The Effect of the Transition to Parenthood on Relationship Quality: An 8-Year Prospective Study," *Journal of Personality and Social Psychology* 96, no. 3 (2009): 601–19; David G. Blanchflower and Andrew Oswald, "Is Well-Being U-Shaped over the Life Cycle?" *Social Science and Medicine, Elsevier* 66, no. 8 (April 2008): 1733–49.

9. RE-CURATE

1. Sigmund Freud, *Three Essays on the Theory of Sexuality*, trans. James Strachey (New York: Basic Books, 1962).

2. Jean Piaget, *The Moral Judgment of the Child* (London: Harcourt, Brace, 1932).

3. Erik H. Erikson, *Childhood and Society* (New York: Norton, 1950).

4. Daniel Levinson, *The Seasons of a Man's Life* (New York: Ballantine, 1978).

5. Roger Gould, *Transformations* (New York: Simon and Schuster, 1978).

6. Bernice Levin Neugarten, *Personality in Middle and Late Life: Empirical Studies* (Redwood City, CA: Atherton Press, 1964).

7. Gail Sheehy, *Passages: Predictable Crises of Adult Life* (New York, Bantam Books, 1974).

8. Levinson, *The Seasons of a Man's Life*.

9. Marshall Goldsmith, *What Got You Here Won't Get You There* (New York: Hachette Books, 2007).

10. Chaim Potok, *In the Beginning* (New York, Fawcett Books, 1975), 9.

10. BUST LOOSE—DISCIPLINE AND LIBERATION

1. Stefan G. Hofmann et al., "The Efficacy of Cognitive-Behavioral Therapy: A Review of Meta-Analyses," *Cognitive Therapy and Research* 36, no. 5 (October 2012): 427–40.

BIBLIOGRAPHY

Arnold, Kara A., Nick Turner, Julian Barling, E. Kevin Kelloway, and Margaret C. McKee. "Transformational Leadership and Psychological Well-Being: The Mediating Role of Meaningful Work." *Journal of Occupational Health Psychology* 12, no. 3 (2007): 193–203.

Blanchflower, David G., and Andrew Oswald. "Is Well-Being U-Shaped over the Life Cycle?" *Social Science and Medicine, Elsevier* 66, no. 8 (April 2008): 1733–49.

Boekaerts, Monique, Moshe Zeidern, and Paul R. Pintrich, *Handbook of Self-Regulation.* San Diego: Academic Press, 2000.

Burke, Ronald J. "Working to Live or Living to Work: Should Individuals and Organizations Care?" *Journal of Business Ethics* 84, Supplement 2 (2009): 167–72.

Childs, Julian H., and Joachim Stoeber. "Do You Want Me to Be Perfect? Two Longitudinal Studies on Socially Prescribed Perfectionism, Stress and Burnout in the Workplace." *Work and Stress* 26, no. 4 (2012): 347–64.

Doss, Brian D., Galena K. Rhoades, Scott M. Stanley, and Howard J. Markman. "The Effect of the Transition to Parenthood on Relationship Quality: An 8-Year Prospective Study." *Journal of Personality and Social Psychology* 96, no. 3 (2009): 601–19.

Erikson, Erik H. *Childhood and Society.* New York: Norton, 1950.

Ferrazzi, Keith, with Tal Raz. *Never Eat Alone and Other Secrets to Success, One Relationship at a Time.* New York: Doubleday, 2005.

Frederickson, Barbara L. "Positive Emotions Broaden and Build." *Advances in Experimental Social Psychology* 47 (2013): 1–53.

Freud, Sigmund. *Three Essays on the Theory of Sexuality.* Translated by James Strachey. New York: Basic Books, 1962.

Gladwell, Malcolm. *Outliers: The Story of Success.* New York: Little Brown and Company, 2008.

Goldsmith, Marshall. *What Got You Here Won't Get You There.* New York: Hachette Books, 2007.

Gould, Roger. *Transformations.* New York: Simon and Schuster, 1978.

Heller, Joseph. *Something Happened.* New York: Ballantine Books, 1974.

Hofmann, Stefan G., Anu Asnaani, Imke J. J. Vonk, Alice T. Sawyer, and Angela Fang. "The Efficacy of Cognitive-Behavioral Therapy: A Review of Meta-Analyses." *Cognitive Therapy and Research* 36, no. 5 (October 2012): 427–40.

Huffington, Arianna. *The Sleep Revolution: Transforming Your Life, One Night at a Time.* New York: Harmony Books, 2016.

Kowalski, Robin M., and Annie McCord. "If I Knew Then What I Know Now: Advice to My Younger Self." *The Journal of Social Psychology* (2019): 1–20.

Kramer, Andrea, and Alton B. Harris. *Breaking Through Bias.* Brookline, MA: Bibliomotion, 2016.

Latham, Gary P., and Gerard Seijts. "Learning Goals or Performance Goals: Is It the Journey or the Destination?" *Ivey Business Journal* (May–June 2006). Retrieved from https://iveybusinessjournal.com/publication/learning-goals-or-performance-goals-is-it-the-journey-or-the-destination/.

Leonard, Kelly, and Tom Yorton. *Yes, And.* New York: Harper Business, 2015.

Levinson, Daniel. *The Seasons of a Man's Life.* New York: Ballantine, 1978.

Loehr, Jim, and Tony Schwartz. *The Power of Full Engagement.* New York: The Free Press, 2003.

Maslow, Abraham H. "A Theory of Human Motivation." *Psychological Review* 50, no. 4 (1943): 370–96.

Neugarten, Bernice Levin. *Personality in Middle and Late Life: Empirical Studies.* Redwood City, CA: Atherton Press, 1964.

Piaget, Jean. *The Moral Judgment of the Child.* London: Harcourt, Brace, 1932.

Porter, Michael E., and Nitin Nohria. "How CEOs Manage Time." *Harvard Business Review* 96, no. 4 (July–August 2018): 42–51.

Potok, Chaim, *In the Beginning.* New York: Fawcett Books, 1975.

Quick, James Campbell, and Lois E. Tetrick (eds.). *Handbook of Occupational Health Psychology* (2nd edition). Washington, DC: American Psychological Association, 2011.

Sheehy, Gail. *Passages: Predictable Crises of Adult Life.* New York: Bantam Books, 1974.

Sin, Nancy L., and Sonja Lyubomirsky. "Enhancing Well-Being and Alleviating Depressive Symptoms with Positive Psychology Interventions: A Practice-Friendly Meta-Analysis." *Journal of Clinical Psychology: In Session* 65, no. 5 (2009): 467–87.

Smith, Eliot R., and Jamie DeCoster. "Dual-Process Models in Social and Cognitive Psychology: Conceptual Integration and Links to Underlying Memory Systems." *Personality and Social Review* 4, no. 2 (2000): 108–31.

Smith, Manuel J. *When I Say No, I Feel Guilty.* New York: Bantam Books, 1975.

Spence, Janet T., and Ann S. Robbins. "Workaholism: Definition, Measurement, and Preliminary Results." *Journal of Personality Assessment* 58, no. 1 (1992): 160–78.

Suls, Jerry, René Martin, and Ladd Wheeler. "Social Comparison: Why, with Whom, and with What Effect?" *Current Directions in Psychological Science* 11, no. 5 (October 2002): 159–63.

Thaler, Richard H., and Cass R. Sunstein. *Nudge: Improving Decisions about Health, Wealth, and Happiness.* New York: Penguin Books, 2008.

Tinsley, Catherine H., and Robin J. Ely. "What Most People Get Wrong about Men and Women: Research Shows the Sexes Aren't So Different." *Harvard Business Review* 96, no. 3 (May–June 2018): 114–21.

Warner, Laura, and Paul Monahan. "Using Audience Commitment to Increase Behavior Changes in Sustainable Landscaping." IFAS Publication Number #WC154. Gainesville: University of Florida Institute of Food and Agricultural Science. Retrieved from: http://edis.ifas.ufl.edu/wc154.

ACKNOWLEDGMENTS

The writing of this book has been a challenging and joyful journey. I am deeply grateful to the many people who have helped me along the way, including:

- My advisors—Eric Brandt, Constance Dierickx, Amy Gordon, David Grossman, Andie Kramer, Joann Lublin, and Sylvia Mendoza
- My book shepherds—Alicia Simons and Erika Heilman
- My agent—Letitia Gomez
- My editors—Suzanne Staszak-Silva and Lara Hahn
- My readers—Tom Bateman, Aaron Golden, Dan Golden, Alex Hartmann, Jim Kelly, and Julie Orbach
- My research advisor—Simon Golden
- My digital strategy consultant—Sarah Collins
- My illustrator—Mary Clare Butler
- My publicist—Tess Woods
- My indexer—Alex Hartmann

READY TO CURATE YOUR LIFE?

Visit Gail at GailGoldenConsulting.com and join her community through the newsletter or find inspiration from her blog.

For performance coaching, organizational transformation, and public speaking, contact Gail directly through email (gail@gailgoldenconsulting.com), on LinkedIn (in/gailgolden), or on Twitter (@GoldenCoach).

INDEX

ABOUT THE AUTHOR

Gail Golden is the principal of Gail Golden Consulting, LLC, a management psychology firm specializing in executive coaching and organizational consultation on leadership development. She earned her PhD in clinical psychology from Indiana University. For the first half of her career, she worked in London, Ontario, where she led a psychotherapy practice, taught in the psychology department and the medical school at Western University, and wrote an advice column in the *London Free Press*. In mid-career she was ready for a new professional challenge, so she went back to school to earn her MBA from Western University. She combined her clinical experience with her business expertise to become a management psychologist in Chicago. In her free time she enjoys entertaining guests, singing, and playing with her grandchildren.